THE SECRET
Sauce

A Recipe To Lead Well and
Get Exceptional Results

DOTTY J BOLLINGER
Ceo Integrity Healthcare Advisors

 FriesenPress

Suite 300 - 990 Fort St
Victoria, BC, V8V 3K2
Canada

www.friesenpress.com

Copyright © 2016 by Dotty J Bollinger
First Edition — 2016

Scripture taken from the Holy Bible, NEW INTERNATIONAL VERSION®. Copyright © 1973, 1978, 1984, 2011 by Biblica, Inc. All rights reserved worldwide. Used by permission. NEW INTERNATIONAL VERSION® and NIV® are registered trademarks of Biblica, Inc. Use of either trademark for the offering of goods or services requires the prior written consent of Biblica US, Inc.

All rights reserved.

No part of this publication may be reproduced in any form, or by any means, electronic or mechanical, including photocopying, recording, or any information browsing, storage, or retrieval system, without permission in writing from FriesenPress.

ISBN
978-1-4602-9521-2 (Hardcover)
978-1-4602-9522-9 (Paperback)
978-1-4602-9523-6 (eBook)

1. BUSINESS & ECONOMICS, WORKPLACE CULTURE

Distributed to the trade by The Ingram Book Company

Table of Contents

Introduction ix

Chapter 1
    Be Real... 1

Chapter 2
    Serve Others... 11

Chapter 3
    Build Your Trust Account.................... 23

Chapter 4
    Measure What Matters........................ 37

Chapter 5
    Model Excellence 45

Chapter 6
    Honor Others 59

Chapter 7
    Praise and Recognize 69

Chapter 8
    Communicate Often and Honestly 85

Chapter 9
    Mentor and Invest............................... 93

Chapter 10
    Hire Well 105

Post Script
    Resist Bone-Headed Strategy............. 119

About The Author 123

I am so grateful for the leaders I've encountered over my more than 35 years in the marketplace, both good and bad. Together, along with my biblical worldview, these folks helped form my point of view on leadership, and as a result I have had the great honor of leading teams to exceptional success. I learned as much from my husband's bosses from his days at Pfizer Pharmaceuticals (experiencing first hand the *life* impact of good and bad bosses), as I did from those who led teams I was a part of. You know who you are, and how grateful I am to have walked a portion of the growth journey with you.

Special thanks to my husband Jim who is my best supporter and my soul mate. And, to our greatest gifts, our children: daughter Ashley, her husband Kevin, and daughter Sara. You are the reason I yearn to make the world a better place to be.

Cover photo credit goes to daughter Ashley. That makes it extra special to me.

Be shepherds of God's flock that is under your care, watching over them—not because you must, but because you are willing, as God wants you to be; not pursuing dishonest gain, but eager to serve.

(1 Peter 5:2)

Introduction

I joined the workforce at the young age of seventeen, taking a job as a nursing assistant in a rest home that cared for twenty or so elderly peoples in need of twenty-four hours a day, seven days per week assistance with activities of daily living. It wasn't my dream job, but it paid well. I liked the old people and the job paid well, so it fit the bill. I showed up on time and when scheduled. I volunteered for extra shifts, and was well liked by the folks I cared for. I picked up the job's duties quickly and competently. I was kind, self-driven, and didn't have to be micro-managed. As a result, I was (what felt like) punished. I was promoted into management without any professional development or experience. I was given a team of nursing assistants that now were under my "control," and I was told to manage and oversee their work. *But how?* I wondered. Without much direction, I resorted to the lessons of my upbringing, drew from my Christian faith, and relied on my common sense and good old-fashioned guesswork. Along with this, I mimicked the best of the leadership under which I had functioned in my short career. An exciting milestone to be certain, but the first of many work situations in which I would find myself without sufficient training and support as I rose up the ladder of management over the next several decades.

Look around at the team you've been assigned to lead. Whether you manage two people or head a company of thousands, these are the people whose lives you are positioned to impact in a significant way each and every day. How you interact with people, guide them, direct them, encourage them, and serve them will directly translate into their level of engagement in the workplace. More significantly, you will impact their overall satisfaction with their particular assignment in life, their sense of self-worth, and, as an extension, their satisfaction with life outside the workplace. Let that settle in. Your performance as a leader directly impacts the lives of those you lead in significant ways. Your assignment is big, it is important, and it is not to be taken lightly.

Think about the jobs that have caused you great anxiety and angst. I'm certain they were associated with a boss that wasn't great, and the stress carried into every aspect of your personal life. Now think about a job you've loved. It's equally likely you had a boss who made you feel empowered, appreciated, and engaged. Even if you brought your job home with you, it was with enthusiasm and excitement about the future and success. Decide right now what kind of leader you want to be as you engage your team. Commit to be the leader that inspires and supports, not the leader who pushes people down.

Great leadership throughout an organization is key to its sustainable success. It is quite simply the secret sauce that many who think themselves business geniuses ignore to their organization's demise. How you treat the people who ultimately will produce the results is key. In this guide, I've broken down key "ingredients" for you to consider, digest, and adopt to drive success for your organization. Follow this recipe. If you do, you can rest well, knowing that you are positively impacting the lives of others and the results of your team.

Anyone can whip a horse to run fast for a short period of time. It takes skill to teach a team to run the long race for sustainable growth and success. Knowing how to be an effective leader isn't knowledge that we're born with. Even the most charismatic personalities need to learn by experience how to honor, respect, motivate, and inspire teams of people who have individual hopes, dreams, and aspirations. In this guide, we'll explore the important ingredients that will make you an effective leader, guiding your team to remarkable results.

I used to think that promoting people without leadership experience or training was a health care organization thing. In my early twenties, I graduated with a nursing degree and quickly found myself in leadership roles. I discovered that competent, smart nurses were often singled out to become charge nurses or head nurses. I witnessed the same promotion strategy with other allied health professionals in the hospitals where I worked. As a result, I thought the industry just didn't worry much about equipping leaders with leadership skills, as long as they were subject matter experts. When I entered the world of corporate business, however, I discovered that the phenomenon is not reserved for health care. It seems common practice to take the best subject-matter qualified people in any position and promote them, with little to no regard for their ability to lead, manage, and inspire the work of others. And then we wonder why many of these previously top performers fail.

Great leadership is the difference between creating a work environment that pays the bills, and one where teammates thrive. It matters in the success of the organization by impacting the satisfaction and engagement of the team, and it inspires creativity, innovation, hard work, dedication, and loyalty. Effective leadership decreases turnover and as such saves money in training and recruiting. Leadership matters from the bottom of an organization to the top. You can't take great care of your customers or deliver a great product if your team isn't engaged and motivated. If you need proof, you only need to look at the exit of a successful leader from an organization to see how a void can impact results. If that leader isn't replaced with one who leads well, the best people and the team engagement and ensuing remarkable results will leave as well.

The Secret Sauce

I've been fortunate along my journey to fashion my leadership style upon experiences with wonderful mentors and inspirational leaders whose behaviors I learned to adopt. Like you, I read lots of books on leadership. I strive to apply the best from all of these sources to inspire, motivate, and serve the teams I lead. I hope this will be a guide that provides a quick but meaty teaching tool for managers who want to lead well and see exceptional results. Whether you're a new leader or an experienced one who is looking for better results, if you model the ingredients of the secret sauce that you'll find in these pages, you'll favorably impact the culture of your team, the efficiency and output of those you lead, and the financial success of your company. And you'll inspire others to do the same as they grow in leadership roles.

Working for an awful boss impacts every aspect of your life. We tend to be keenly aware of the magnitude of leadership on our lives when we work for bad leaders. Leading well can also have a dynamically positive impact the lives of those we lead. Your level of enjoyment for what you do for a living will by design have a profound impact on your home life as well. If great leadership ultimately improves a highly engaged teammate's satisfaction outside the workplace as well, that's quite an honor. You hold within your positional authority the ability to improve the lives of those within your scope of influence. You also have the ability to make others' lives miserable. Lead well and you'll experience the satisfaction and appreciation of a team who knows they are respected, honored, and served. Consider the impact of your every word and action on the people you lead and the customers you serve.

I had a memorable boss at a law firm many years ago. She came into the office at about noon each day and stayed as late as her cases required. She expected each associate to stay as late as she stayed. The associates called her "Night Shift Mary." As associates, urban legend says we were expected to be the first in and the last out of the office each day. Since Night Shift Mary didn't begin her day until we younger staffers were five hours into ours, we felt neither valued nor respected. After all, we had to stay our ten hours plus hers. Mary had a very high turnover rate on her team, as associates simply put in their time until a better position came along. I always remembered Night Shift Mary's example throughout my career, and I made certain people knew exactly what I expected of them and why, and how my own actions did or did not reflect what I expected them to be doing.

Just as Mary impacted me, so too did the best leader I ever had the privilege of working with. He left me with a great example of what intentional, authentic leadership looks like. This leader, I'll call him Matt, was always teaching, encouraging, and pushing his team to stretch their belief in themselves. He established expectations that set a high bar for our delivery of results. We always felt like he was in the effort with us. We always felt supported. Matt made his team believe they could do more than they'd done before. We not only believed it ... we delivered more. Day after day after day. Matt honored us, believed in us, taught us, supported us, and made us feel like we were making him proud with our efforts.

Strive to become a leader that people want to follow. Think about experiences that you've had that motivated you. Also think about times when you felt unappreciated and uninspired. People talk about the impact of great and awful leaders upon their job satisfaction for years. Become the great boss that people talk about and remember. Become the boss whose style they emulate as they move up the management ladder. Become the one they tell their family and friends about. Become the reason people love what they do each and every day.

Anyone can learn to lead well, regardless of age, education, or experience. Great leadership is contagious. It's hard for other people in management positions around you to carry out a dictatorial leadership style when your team loves the culture your leadership inspires. You'll not only impact your team, but you'll make a huge impact on the culture of your workplace as a whole. There is no greater assignment than to lead others. Desiring to do it well is the important first step in understanding that leadership matters and is a skill to be honed.

It is an honor to lead another to a higher place. When you lead, you impact the emotional and physical experience of those around you for good or for bad. Edify. Build people up. Protect. Teach. Block and tackle. Clear the path. Inspire. Encourage. Sacrifice. And do it again and again and again to ensure the team feels valued, appreciated, and challenged. Then step back and watch what happens. Lead well and get exceptional results.

Chapter 1
Be Real

> **COMMIT** *to sharing yourself with other people in genuine, relational, authentic ways.*

A friend from the restaurant management world once shared a great if not obvious insight with me. "You can have the best marketing plan in the world to launch a new restaurant chain," she said, "but if the food isn't good, it won't matter." Quite a simple if not obvious thought, but one that reminds me of an important leadership truth as well. Leading well can't cure bone-headed business decisions made outside your control, but bad leadership can ruin a business that's running well, and prevent growth in a business that has potential. Ultimately, great leaders understand they must motivate people to deliver exceptional results *and* use the same skills and principles to help set the right course for their organization.

Leadership matters. As a healthcare consultant I work with numerous teams at once and I see time and time again practices that have great physicians, excellent medicine, teammates focused on delivering good care, and even fairly sound back office procedures. But in the absence of great leadership, a practice won't grow. It simply limps along, barely getting the job done, with average employee engagement, average customer satisfaction, and flat financial results. As I help teams find the right leadership structure for each group, I search for people who possess the ingredients of the secret sauce of leadership. Only then will teams fully engage and deliver extraordinary results.

Great leaders are comfortable in their own skin and comfortable being real with people they seek to lead and inspire. Don't confuse this ingredient of authenticity with building friendships. Friendships include informal agreements between two or more people to support each other in good times and in bad. Your authenticity or willingness to be real in your role as a leader is for the purpose of letting people understand what makes you tick so they can trust you and follow your lead. As you consider revealing your authentic, real self to your teammates, think about it in terms of building strong relationships of confidence and trust.

I worked with a CFO who is one of my favorite leaders and an unusual place to find this first

The Secret Sauce

ingredient of the secret sauce. I say unusual because the CFO stereotype wouldn't generally attribute strong people skills to c-suite financial folks. This leader is different. He genuinely loves his team. He appreciates his team's hard work and dedication, and he isn't afraid to show gratitude in tangible ways. This CFO reveals his authentic self with his team by the stories he shares and actions he takes. He opens himself up by daring to share of himself.

At Thanksgiving, his wife brings in fancy baked goods for the entire staff, sometimes even with their children in tow. This leader, his wife, and his kids walk the cubicle aisles handing out delicious holiday treats to each teammate. This leader grew to be a top executive, and he never forgot how he got there. The work of his team lifted him up. By sharing his family and his gratitude with his team, he showed the team that he honored and appreciated them. He was humble, and he showed the team with this tangible exercise not only that he appreciates them, but also that he trusts them enough to share his heart of gratitude and his family.

> Your willingness to reveal your genuine self is an important step to building trust and care.

His team loved and respected him. Most importantly, they loved their jobs. They showed great devotion to him, and in times of discord within the organization, they trusted him to be a beacon of light to follow. This simple act of gratitude to his team is a special ingredient of his leadership style. As members of the team were promoted to different jobs, this was an act they remembered, and some even adopted this ritual as their own. It wasn't unusual to see these younger leaders share the gift of their family and simple acts of thanks as they walked the cubicles of their new teams.

It's simple. The first ingredient of the secret sauce is leadership delivered by people who aren't afraid to be real. We all know *real* when we see it—people who aren't afraid to take off the mask and genuinely reveal themselves as they seek to engage with us. This level of authenticity may take time, effort, a humble spirit, and hard work. You can't fake it, but if you want to drive results as well as improve the lives of those you lead, you'll need to commit to being real with the people around you. Your willingness to reveal your genuine self is an important step to building trust and care.

> Anything that reveals a brief look beyond the title will humanize you to the people you lead and open a door for an authentic connection.

Perhaps this isn't a comfortable place for you to begin. If so, start simple. Your workspace is a perfect place to tell people who you are and to share a part of your story. Personalize your space with a few things that indicate who you really are—drawings from your children, a *Star Trek* mug, or even a picture of the last team you led. Anything that reveals a brief look

The Secret Sauce

beyond the title will humanize you to the people you lead and open a door for an authentic connection. You'll learn a lot about your team by noticing their workspace as well, so take the time to look and engage in conversation about what you see. Ask questions about the pictures. You'll also learn who might not be engaged in the workplace. I always let my team know that if their offices were sparse, I saw this as a potential sign of lack of commitment. In other words, if you can pack up and leave in thirty seconds because you never unpacked your personal belongings, you may not have unpacked your emotional commitment to the job either, and might not be in it for the long haul.

Your actions need to match your words. Whether you are new or experienced in the workplace, you have a great story to tell. Along with telling a story with your workspace, you also have several great stories to tell that have molded who you are.

Some of these stories will inspire others and will be key to helping you make a positive impact on your team. Take time to frame these narratives and even practice them with someone you trust (sort of a "focus group" to gauge the impact of the story). From moment one your team is forming an opinion about what kind of leader you're going to be—from your facial expressions, to your communication style, to your actions. Your stories and anecdotes

> Being authentic means revealing the right things at the right time to the right audience.

will help fill in the blanks as people form opinions and match what they see with what they hear. Even if you aren't a new leader to your team but are striving to be a better leader, stories will help to frame your transition and growth intentions. In this case, you may tell a story about why you are striving to change your leadership style. Using true, real stories that match your actions will show your team that you are authentic.

How "real" is right? I had a boss once who on more than one occasion thanked his team for their hard work and dedication in very genuine ways during team events. Sometimes he would even get choked up, which was a great show of vulnerability and authenticity. He would also add how much he appreciated the positive financial impact his team's hard work had on his family and their standard of living. He genuinely appreciated that the team made him rich, but I know that he lost the team every time with that overture. At that point in the delivery of gratitude, each listener was thinking about the disconnect between their own wealth and his, and comparing the contribution and hard work they'd made as compared to what they perceived his contribution to be.

This moment of authenticity actually took away from motivating the team. Being authentic means revealing the right things at the right time to the right audience.

> Take thirty minutes at the end of a day and informally connect with your team.

One effective way to connect with your team on a personal level is during informal get-togethers.

The Secret Sauce

These don't have to take place outside the workplace, but they should create opportunities for people to put down their work and focus on real connections with the people they're working with and for. Perhaps take thirty minutes at the end of a day and informally connect with your team. Bring a cake or a cheese platter and punch or wine if your workplace allows. Break the ice to get people talking about topics other than work. Some of the most beneficial connections that build loyalty and team engagement are these informal, "real" gatherings.

My team held monthly Friday afternoon get-togethers when we would share a glass of wine and just talk about non-work related subjects. Sometimes we'd learn a new skill (someone would share their wine knowledge, for example), and other times we'd just chat. For thirty minutes once a month we would stand together in a room with no agenda except to get to know each other better. People appreciated those gatherings and connected in important ways. This simple "meeting" showed people that they mattered, and that personal connection was important and valued by the organization. It revealed care. People generally are motivated by actions that tell them they are worth the time. And, it challenged all of us to be authentic.

> Be real, dare to thoughtfully reveal yourself to people, and consider the impact of whatever it is that you're choosing to share upon the listener.

Not everyone is going to like being real. When I entered the workforce over thirty years ago, one of the first things I was told was, "Leave your personal life at the door." It took me years to recognize that this was very wrong advice. Some of the people you lead may feel like that remains sound policy. When you are authentic, it creates a culture where authenticity is valued. Not everyone will want to open up and share about him or herself. Likewise, some won't want to know things about you. As you practice revealing your real self in the workplace, you may encounter people who simply don't approve of or respect this ingredient. That's ok. We'll discuss motivating folks who just aren't interested in participating in making the secret sauce in a later chapter.

Be real, dare to thoughtfully and respectfully reveal yourself to people, and consider the impact of whatever it is that you're choosing to share upon the listener. Everything you reveal should instill confidence to the receiver of the information. Your authenticity will inspire people to work hard and be loyal. Because they know you care about them enough to let your guard down, they will work hard to deliver exceptional results. We follow people we respect, and we respect people who trust us enough to open up about themselves. Being real will help you to become a leader who makes a positive impact on the lives of the people you lead.

The Secret Sauce

"Do nothing out of selfish ambition or vain conceit. Rather, in humility value others above yourselves …"

Philippians 2:3.

Chapter 2
Serve Others

> *Commit to serving others. Imagine the impact of people knowing you desire to* **SERVE** *them more than you are concerned with them serving you.*

Servant leadership takes humility, commitment, and care. A servant heart is sacrificial. It puts others' needs above its own. It will be time consuming and it's nearly impossible to fake. I once worked with a leader who was highly educated and well put together. He wore expensive suits, always had a smile on his face, and often came bearing simple, unique, and thoughtful gifts for those around him in the workplace. His demeanor was professional yet kind, generous, and positive. He quite simply seemed too good to be true! Even his biggest fans wondered if he was sincere or playing a game for personal gain. And then Thanksgiving came around.

I learned that he and his family stayed up all night preparing goodies that were staples of any fancy Thanksgiving feast, like turkeys filled with delicious stuffing, and homemade pies. At daylight he delivered these goodies to the homes of every member of his team. Sacrifice and care delivered with every delicious bite. He could have delivered trays from the local deli, but he didn't. He and his family gave of their time and talents and chose sacrifice over self. As you might imagine, his team loved him. They were devoted and loyal to him, and they followed his lead by being engaged in the organization. If you asked his team if they liked their jobs, they would assure you with a resounding, "We love our jobs!" And they loved and appreciated their servant leader.

> One of the easiest ways to measure your servant leadership is to think about a job you've left. Who stayed connected to you?

How do you gauge your natural servant-heart aptitude? One of the easiest ways to measure your servant leadership is to think about a job you've left. Who stayed connected to you? Did anyone want to follow you to your new place of employment? Do any of your prior teammates stay connected to you on social media? If the answer is "no" to these questions, you might need some practice in serving others from

The Secret Sauce

a place of leadership. Servant leaders garner relational bonds that withstand the confines of specific positions. Serving others leaves a mark on the people you've served, and they don't forget you. When you receive a phone call from a teammate you led years earlier asking you for informal guidance and direction in their current situation, you'll know you did it right.

"Serving" is anything you do as a leader to support your team's success. This can be as small and as hands-on as assisting with tasks, or as big and as ground-breaking as facilitating an important process change that removes barriers to success. I remember as a young nursing leader on one of my first days in management my team was particularly overwhelmed with a record number of patients. We were short staffed due to sick call-ins. I had my own set of responsibilities as nurse manager that needed to be completed that day; however, I could see that my team was going to have an awful day, which would impact negatively upon the patients in our care. I knew I needed to do something to relieve the pressure valve that being short staffed had created. On this particular day, I simply jumped in and starting doing tasks. There were beds to be made for patients who were off the unit for physical therapy. I didn't send up a flare or make an announcement; I simply grabbed clean linen and started making beds. I wasn't being strategic with this move; I was simply jumping in to help where I could see I could make a

> "Serving" is anything you do as a leader to support your team's success.

quick difference to the team. I was absolutely astounded by their response. The temperament of this frazzled team on this busy day immediately changed. It was as if seeing the leader willing to jump in and help with the more menial tasks sent a strong message that, "We're all in this together." Older more experienced nurses who had been skeptical of a young nurse being promoted were impressed with my willingness to pitch in. I made a few beds, and my worst detractors now gave me a second look. That day I earned respect. This was my first experience seeing the significant impact servant leadership can deliver. It wouldn't be my last.

> It was as if seeing the leader willing to jump in and help with the more menial tasks sent a strong message that, "We're all in this together."

Pitching in and doing the task is the simple example, but frankly one that too many leaders think is beneath them. Imagine the impact to your team if you are a call center manager and you answer a few calls on a busy day. This simple act won't eliminate the stress of the day, but it will send a powerful message that will speak volumes to the team. Assisting with simple tasks shows you care. It keeps you humble and tells the team you consider all tasks important. Think about ways you might step in and relieve the stress of the team in tangible, hands-on ways to show your servant heart.

One of your most important responsibilities is to break down barriers that are inhibiting the team's success. There are deliverables to be produced, as well as goals, and objectives your team is expected to meet. A good leader knows what barriers are preventing the team's success and which ones can be controlled or removed. You won't have to guess – your teammates know exactly what the barriers are. Once identified, empower and lead the group to innovative thinking for the purpose of problem solving. Together, find the right solutions, and guide the team to overcome those roadblocks. Serving others includes guiding them and encouraging them to problem solve.

Other barriers may be outside the team's control. For example, most organizations can expect some type of political discord within the ranks. Sometimes the biggest barrier to your team's success is the "heat" that comes down from up the ladder. When you take the heat, protecting the team from the distractions that go with political pressures within the organization, you remove a barrier that the team will never know even exists. Political landmines can be set by people who don't even recognize the negative impact of their actions. A wise servant leader recognizes these distractions for what they are—just distractions and barriers to success. Instead of reorganizing workflow to accommodate the distraction, do everything within your power to eliminate the distraction while your team continues with their daily duties in a distraction-free environment. For example,

> One of your most important responsibilities is to break down barriers that are inhibiting the team's success.

if someone up the ladder is asking for time consuming meetings and reports that are creating such an imposition on your team's time that getting their actual job done is in jeopardy, take on the communication responsibility yourself. The person above has a desire for improved information, and you must be the person to satisfy that need so your team members can do their jobs. Identify the reason for the information request and create an information sharing opportunity that is not disruptive to the team's efficiency. People who demand reams of reports generally have a desire to understand a process better. Take the time to ask probing questions to determine the actual need, and then help them get the knowledge they desire. Creating reports that ultimately no one reads is a waste of everyone's time and impacts the efficiency of the report producer. By saving precious time, you will take away a barrier to success and serve your team well.

Servant leaders seek input from the team. Your team will know exactly what makes their jobs difficult. It's up to you to know how that perceived barrier fits into the larger picture of the organization, and whether or not it can be corrected. One example that quickly comes to mind is Internet speed. Perhaps you're managing teams that spend a lot of downtime waiting for the screen to move through their software program. If the Internet capacity were improved, the

> Servant leaders make tough calls for the good of the team.

wait between screens would eliminate a lot of frustrating, wasted downtime. In reality, you probably can't fix the Internet speed. But you can make certain the people with the authority to approve the budget for upgrades to the system know about the downtime. You also can help with maximizing the organization of the workflow. Help the team problem-solve how work could be redistributed and reorganized to make use of the "between-screen-wait-time." Ensure the team understands what the long-term fix plan is, and the timeline for that fix. Serve the team by validating their frustrations, helping to implement a change in work flow by seeing the big picture, and reassuring them that an improved fix is on the way.

Servant leaders make tough calls for the good of the team. Some people won't be engaged, won't give their best, or won't care about the success of the team and the organization. Servant leadership won't always inspire the un-inspirable to excel, engage, or act with integrity. People who don't pull their weight or who are bad for the culture of your team are barriers to the team's success. You'll need to be genuine in your assessment of team members' abilities, and then support, drive, mentor, or exit these folks appropriately. Serving others doesn't mean that you lower the standards for what success looks like in your organization. It means you give timely, honest assessments of performance. You guide and mentor those who are determined to improve.

> Lowering standards is counterproductive to serving the team. Instead, you must commit to exit teammates who aren't willing to get onboard and work with full effort to properly meet expectations and drive results. These aren't always low performers. These could be some of your best performers who, unfortunately, are delivering results without integrity.

Lowering standards is counterproductive to serving the team. Instead, you must commit to exit teammates who aren't willing to get onboard and work with full effort to properly meet expectations and drive results. These aren't always low performers. These could be some of your best performers who, unfortunately, are delivering results without integrity. Perhaps they are breaking ethical rules to be successful. Every time you exit a teammate who takes shortcuts on integrity but is delivering results, you gain additional respect from your team. The team knows the bad acts of others, and they know the gamers of a reward system that allows a bad actor to become a rewarded top performer. Your willingness to lose the results gained by unethical practices will show your team you are genuinely committed to the integrity and long-term well being of the organization. They'll work even harder to make up for the bad actor's lost production. It also sends a quick and simple message that your servant heart is an asset of strength for the team and should not be mistaken for weakness. Anyone else

The Secret Sauce

thinking the shortcut is the better way to go will learn a valuable lesson.

Leading others well by serving them is an important ingredient of the secret sauce that drives the most successful organizations. Imagine the efforts of a workforce of individuals who know you care about them enough to serve them by building them up, clearing the path of barriers, encouraging them, guiding them, investing in them, and believing in them, and exiting those who don't belong.

"Do unto others as you would have them do unto you." That's where the servant heart comes from. Practice servant leadership. It will make you special as a leader and different from most of the rest of the world. You are the person that your team is talking about to their loved ones at the dinner table at night. What are they saying about you? Are they telling stories of how you served them and the organization? Or are they talking about your lack of understanding of their plight? It's an honor to serve others and doing so will inspire productivity that delivers exceptional results. Practice serving until it becomes your natural approach to leader your team. You'll find the more you serve, the more your team will respond in a positive way.

> Practice serving until it becomes your natural approach to leading your team. You'll find the more you serve, the more your team will respond in a positive way.

I love the concept of serving one another in the workplace. Culturally it matches a biblical worldview. While authors have written about the servant leadership style for decades, this "style" is really based on the oldest biblical principle, "Do unto others as you would have them do unto you." Serving others is a heart choice and a leadership ingredient you can adopt at any time. Unfortunately, many people in positions of power think in terms of manipulating team performance for the purpose of gaining financial success or meeting organizational goals for personal gain. That is a shortsighted management style that is far too common in our churn and burn, self-centered world. When we serve others first, we show a heart of humility, understanding, and care. People in turn respond by being highly engaged and enthusiastic about their jobs. They display incredible drive and profound loyalty. And they proudly deliver exceptional results.

> "A generous person will prosper; whoever refreshes others will be refreshed,"
>
> Proverbs 11:25.

Chapter 3
Build Your Trust Account

> *Commit to earning* **TRUST**. *Everything you do either builds up or depletes your trust account.*

As a hospital critical care nurse, I was assigned to the crash team—a team of trained healthcare professionals who would respond to incidents anywhere in the hospital where a patient "arrested" and required CPR and resuscitation measures. As a critical care nurse, dealing with life and death situations was what I was trained to do. It was, respectfully, routine. When a patient outside the critical care unit arrested, we would hear a special announcement on the PA system overhead, and off the crash team would go running. We were running, but we weren't anxious. We had a job to do, and we were well trained to do it.

I will never forget the expressions on the faces of the nurses on the scene when the crash team arrived. These were nurses who didn't customarily deal with emergency situations. They were scared to death and feeling out of their expertise delivering resuscitation measures. The instant they saw the crash team running down the hallway, they knew we were about to take control. We could tangibly see the relief wash over their faces and the fear and anxiety leave them. The crash team would swoop in, take over the resuscitation efforts, and quite often revive the crashing patient and stabilize them for transfer to critical care.

> Anyone can cheerlead and guide teammates in times of prosperity, but great leaders inspire teams to deliver results in spite of adversity.

I like to think of that crash team, while acting quickly with skill and competence, as ducks. We were a fury of action, but what you saw was calm, competent interventions. Because the crash team remained calm, everyone involved in the situation settled down and believed the situation was under control. The power of remaining focused and confident immediately calmed the anxiety of everyone involved. Calm leadership in the midst of an emergency didn't change the gravity of the medical condition, the need for immediate intervention, or the fact that a life was on the line. Rather, it kept the environment free of chaos and allowed for life saving measures to be implemented calmly, methodically, and without the confusion that an environment filled with chaos would drive. Calm leadership builds team confidence and trust. Hair-on-fire leadership erodes it.

Every workplace will encounter challenges and obstacles on a daily basis. One of the best measurements of leading well is how you guide, encourage, and inspire a team through those difficult times. Anyone can cheerlead and guide teammates in times of prosperity, but great leaders inspire teams to deliver results in spite of adversity. The best scenario is leading through adversity in a manner that makes the team strong and where the full extent of the challenge is known to you but not to necessarily to everyone around you. When you lead a team through choppy waters and the team thinks the waters were just a little rough, you've led well. Ultimately success or failure will be attributed once you get to the other side by how you lead the team to results in spite of adversity.

Your team will adopt your vision of what lies ahead. If you exhibit behavior that indicates the sky is falling, then your team will follow your lead and believe the sky is falling. Likewise, if you believe there's a great challenge coming that the team is ready for and capable of overcoming, the team will believe that as well. Quite simply, we rarely

> I'm a firm believer that people would prefer to be part of a solution rather than ranting and worrying about the problem.

exceed our own expectations. Fear and anxiety set up any team for failure as they focus on the obstacle instead of the goals. Your leadership sets the course for the team's expectations and ultimately determines the results. It's a rare challenge that can't be overcome. It's also a rare challenge that a deep breath and a new strategy can't improve. Allowing an entire group of people to get upset and anxious about a situation that has a solution doesn't move the organization forward. I'm a firm believer that people would prefer to be part of a solution rather than ranting and worrying about the problem.

> See every frustration and challenge as an opportunity to improve your team, build confidence in your leadership, and build the value in your team "trust" account.

In some industries, an unscheduled visit from regulators is an expected (if not pleasant) occurrence. How leaders lead through these important and necessary detractors of time in the workplace is a great example of being able to lead well through times of stress and anxiety. Working in licensed healthcare organizations, we always knew what rules and regulations we needed to operate under, and we always did our best to act accordingly. We trained, prepped, and executed our daily work with an effort to exceed the quality required by law. In other words, we never had to worry that we weren't in compliance with the requisite rules and regulations, because we

The Secret Sauce

exceeded the requirements every day. Still, when the state regulators unexpectedly knocked on the door, there was a tendency for anxiety levels to go through the roof. But there was also an opportunity to be the calm in the midst of the storm. Often, all that was required to diffuse the high stress of the situation was a quick team huddle, with reminders that we were ready for the survey. A call to action to "just do what you do every day" went a long way to ensuring the team remained confident, calm, and focused as the surveyors followed them around and reviewed their work.

There are daily opportunities to be frustrated in any job and in any workplace. Calmly handling adversity is a necessary ingredient in the secret sauce. Most frustrations will be easy to resolve, requiring a balance between common sense and competent intervention. Sometimes frustrations will involve uncovering something that is genuinely wrong. While these are two very different scenarios, how you react to either situation dictates the level of confidence your team will have in your ability to lead through times of trouble. Calmly handling the day-to-day frustrations with maturity and competence will allow you to have the full faith and trust of your team if and when the bad thing happens. See every frustration and challenge as an opportunity to improve your team, build

> Confident leadership doesn't get frazzled. Every challenge is simply an opportunity to shine.

confidence in your leadership, and build the value in your team "trust" account. As you've built relationships with authenticity and earned their respect as you've served them, your team will see you as a beacon of light that can be trusted to lead them safely through challenges. Your trust account is a key asset to your team's sustainable success.

People like to be around other people who are calm, in control, confident, and who exude a peaceful affect. Confident leadership doesn't get frazzled. Every challenge is simply an opportunity to shine. Even if you uncover an injustice worthy of righteous indignation, you still should not exhibit frenzy. As the leader, you set the emotional temperature gauge for your team. If you are negative, your team will be negative. Likewise, if you are positive and have a "can do" attitude, your team will follow accordingly. Either way, your team will be looking to you to set the stage. They will look to you to gain confidence that a solution is available and that success is possible. This doesn't mean that you minimize serious situations. It means you lead calmly and competently through times of adversity and trouble.

> Anyone can manage a group of people when there are no challenges and roadblocks, but inspiring groups of people to deliver excellence in times of trouble takes significant skill.

You're going to have your share of work stress, pressure, and opportunities to get frazzled. How you react in these situations will have a huge impact on the satisfaction and productivity of your team. Your ability to remain calm when the pressure rises will directly impact your team's ability to do the same. More importantly, it will have a direct correlation on your team's ability to exceed expectations when times are tough. Anyone can manage a group of people when there are no challenges and roadblocks, but inspiring groups of people to deliver excellence in times of trouble takes significant skill. Practice leading well in small challenges to ensure you can be ready when the big challenge comes.

Be conscious of your words, tone, and facial expressions. Ensure that you are exuding confidence, clearly communicating direction, asking for team insights, and offering assurance that challenges will successfully be overcome.

> Recognize and reward those who follow your lead and emulate steady behavior.

We can all think of people we've worked with who couldn't wait to spread the news to others that "the sky is falling!" After all, misery loves company. Many people don't want to be alone as they head for cover. For these chaos promoters, as the frenzy spreads, all energy is pointed towards elevating anxiety and implementing self-preservation mechanisms. After all, the sky is falling! The sky is falling! I like to call these people "the ones with their hair on fire." You've met them. They find an injustice or wrongdoing, and instead of strategizing the corrective action, they would prefer to get everyone thinking the end of the world is surely near. While this approach may be consistent with a desire to bang our fists on the table and fight injustice, it does little to build confidence and trust within the team. Recognize and reward those who follow your lead and emulate steady behavior. For those who have more difficulty remaining calm in the midst of the storm, provide one on one coaching and offer additional encouragement. Manage hair on fire behavior quickly, as it's contagious and will quickly undo the peace you're trying hard to build with the team.

Is there anything more peaceful than watching a duck swim gracefully across the top of peaceful lake water? Gliding like dancers, they move in groups with cooperation and grace. That's what you see on top of the water. But look under the water and their little webbed feet are paddling a mile a minute, hidden from anyone except those closest to them, taking them in the right direction, steering them toward the goal. You are going to have numerous opportunities to be panicked or annoyed. In some workplaces, you'll have these opportunities every day. In these situations, it will benefit you to "be the duck." Keeping the vision of the duck in your mind is a good way to remind yourself that no matter what you encounter, you must remain calm.

> Calmly notify the right people and lead the team to begin the correction process.

Perhaps your boss has moved up the time a key assignment is due from tomorrow to today. What do you do? You have two options. One, you can run around your

The Secret Sauce

team area and scream, "It's got to be done today! It's got to be done today!" The second option is to gather together key team members who are working on the assignment and calmly ask them what resources they need to accomplish the task within a shortened delivery schedule.

Perhaps you're auditing team processes and you find evidence that a key part of a procedure has been done incorrectly. You discover it's been done incorrectly for a very long time. What do you do? You have two options. One, you can throw up your arms and scream that everyone around you is stupid and "We're all going down!" The second option is to determine what, if anything needs to be changed immediately, and what corrective plan must be implemented to correct past wrongs. Calmly notify the right people and lead the team to begin the correction process.

How you react to difficult situations sets the tone for all those around you and is perhaps the best indicator of your capacity to lead well. It requires emotional stability. As you go, so your team will go. Choose the calm and steady path. You will likely encounter

> In any difficulty, people innately wonder how the situation will impact them personally. As a result, the team will look to you as their barometer. Will they be okay after this storm passes? How you react to correct the situation may well impact the livelihood of your team or the company as a whole.

opportunities every day in which you can react with frenzy or lead with grace. These might involve anything from employee discord, policy challenges that need to be implemented yesterday, process hiccups due to obstacles outside your control, and everything in-between. When the team trusts your leadership, you will have extra breathing room to figure out next steps. You all benefit. When the team knows they can rely on your leadership and guidance, you'll benefit by gaining the gift of *time* to figure out the situation. When people trust you to lead them effectively through adversity, they aren't concerned with you acting quickly. Conversely, if your team doesn't have confidence in you, their anxiety level is escalated and they want to know, "Quick—what's next? What's next?" After all, their hair will be on fire!

The team needs calm leadership more in times of trouble than at any other time. Personal safety and security are primal human needs.[1] In any difficulty, people innately wonder how the situation will impact them personally. As a result, the team will look to you as their barometer. Will they be okay after this storm passes? How you react to correct the situation may well impact the livelihood of your team or the company as a whole. When leaders display behavior indicating the sky is falling, it puts these basic foundational needs in jeopardy for everyone involved. Remaining calm and emotionally mature during times of difficulty doesn't mean you are indicating

---

1   A.H. Maslow, "A Theory of Human Motivation," *Psychological Review* 50 (4) (1943): 370–396.

The Secret Sauce

you are okay with what's going wrong. It simply means you understand your responsibility to lead, and you are choosing to display quiet strength as you work to resolve the issue. Providing calm, competent, strong, confident leadership and direction will provide your team with the trust and confidence that you will lead them to the right track and towards an ultimate solution.

Likewise, the team needs to know that you understand the challenge, understand accurately the gravity of the situation, and that you are doing something about it. Communicating with confidence in a calm manner will allow your team to move forward while believing that you're taking care of business. You'll need to find the right balance between communicating your plan with enough specificity to ensure the team that you're handling it, but without enough specificity to endanger the organization or the individuals involved. This is a delicate balance that will require you to be a subject matter expert regarding the situation, or to bring in someone who has that level of competence. This simply means it's up to you to determine the gravity of the opportunity, and then communicating or not communicating, depending on what you're dealing with. An employee challenge may require confidential counseling and resolution. Likewise, a compliance situation may require you to contact your legal department, and resolution will be largely invisible to many on the team. Because you've calmly led the team through challenges, they'll trust your actions and know you'll communicate as you are able.

> Recognize that how you lead through any situation is contagious. Encourage, cheerlead, strategize, reward, recognize, and build up during times of adversity.

There may come a time when the barrier is too big to overcome using usual strategies. Sometimes the worst thing does happen. Because you've led well in the small, daily challenges, you'll see your team well engaged and following your lead. You will lead the group to find a solution, with team engagement and dedication intact. It doesn't ensure a successful resolution, but it does ensure that the best efforts will be dedicated to it.

Leading with calm maturity doesn't mean withholding key information. It means delivering key information with an air of confidence so that people understand the facts of the situation, but they trust in your leadership to get them through it. Be respectful, honest, and encouraging. Recognize that how you lead through any situation is contagious. Encourage, cheerlead, strategize, reward, recognize, and build up during times of adversity.

Trust is an important ingredient in the secret sauce. Leading calmly and purposefully and inspiring others to do the same builds your trust account. Think of every interaction as an opportunity to earn the trust of people who will in turn produce exceptional results.

The Secret Sauce

"They did not require an accounting from those to whom they gave the money to pay the workers, because they acted with complete honesty,"

2 Kings 12:15.

Chapter 4
Measure What Matters

> *Commit to* **UNDERSTANDING** *what metrics really matter, measure them in meaningful ways, and keep it simple.*

All of us model and recalibrate our behavior based on key performance indicators. Our children strive to bring home "As" on report cards, we run for a faster time in a 5K, we look at our speedometer when driving in the school zone to ensure that we slow down, and we even step on the bathroom scale each morning to see if we've gained weight. We're geared to measure success by data points in everything we do, and in this world of supercharged technology, the ability to gather and digest data is everywhere. Making certain we pay attention to what really matters is an important ingredient in leading well.

Key performance indicators (or KPIs) are those things that any organization measures in order to determine success. Each individual teammate and each team as a whole has KPIs that must be met in order for the organization to be successful. One of your most important responsibilities is accurately determining which KPIs are the right indicators of your team's success, and which ones they have the biggest ability to influence as they complete their work. Understanding what to measure and when to measure it is a key ingredient in the secret sauce.

One trap many leaders fall into is measuring too much, focusing on too many areas, and being paralyzed by data without actually having any of the information they need to successfully impact the results of the business. Keep it simple for the benefit of your team and for your ultimate success. Find three to seven key performance indicators that your team can impact directly, measure accurately, set goals around, and be rewarded for when they are met.

Determining what to measure is key. Essentially, you are striving to reduce your team's performance to metrics and key performance indicators to create an objective way to measure results. People are emotional beings and sometimes prefer measuring success in subjective formats; however, there is always an objective way to measure any effort. For example, customer satisfaction might seem on the surface to

The Secret Sauce

be a subjective measurement—more emotion than statistics. However, satisfaction is easily measured mathematically, by survey response, repeat visits, word of mouth referrals, or other measurable means. While your gut reaction might be that satisfaction is an attempt to measure a subjective feeling, that feeling translates into measurable actions.

> Measure what will help you improve tomorrow's performance over yesterday's.

It's important that you measure the team's output in terms the team understands so that you are speaking a common language, effectively communicating performance, and making corrections. If you can't measure something, then it's difficult to know the business impact of your team's performance. Know what your team is expected to produce as a part of the entire organization's success. Then, identify the key measures that will show your team is effectively producing those results., and most importantly which actions are effectively pulling the levers.

Monitor KPIs that are critical to your business and its success. Spend your time here, as it will be the most important time you invest in understanding your team's performance. You need to find KPIs that can be measured efficiently. Notice I did not say "easily," as you may not currently have easy access to the data. Once you have identified a KPI, create a standard, which includes a definition of what the KPI means and exactly how you will measure this. Look for benchmarks. Depending on your business, you may be able to benchmark against an industry standard, or you may not have that capability and will instead benchmark against your team's prior performance. Either strategy works. Your goal is simple. Measure what will help you improve tomorrow's performance over yesterday's.

> As you create strategy and react to internal and external factors on team performance, you need a baseline of measurable indicators to accurately understand the impact of process change on your business.

Other than measuring current performance, there are many reasons why teams need to measure specific metrics. As you create strategy and react to internal and external factors on team performance, you need a baseline of measurable indicators to accurately understand the impact of change on your business. If you implement process changes, whether material or superficial, and whether based on analytics or gut intuition, only accurate measurement will allow you to completely understand the change's impact upon your business. Many new managers make this mistake. They implement change and have no way of knowing if it was successful. Follow your metrics and keep track of business changes. You should be able to see a result from any action that you take. Additionally, when you make a change, you need to set a time when you will make a decision to modify the change, endorse the change, or abort the change. This decision should be predefined prior to implementing the change.

Beware of making multiple changes at once. It's tempting for new leaders to step in and make swooping changes in several different areas. Unless you know what the baseline is, and how each individual change impacts performance, you may move the business forward, but not predictably or sustainably. If the business starts to face challenges, which new process might have caused it? If the business soars, which implementation was responsible? If you know this answer, then you can eliminate won't doesn't work and focus on what does. This doesn't mean you need to go slow and not take chances, but it does mean you need a vision for action and monitoring that makes sense. This is important for your team. It will be important that the team understands both the vision and the results tied to actions through measurement.

Once a metric is "perfected," find another metric to measure as you continuously improve the performance of the team. I've seen challenges that required implementation of a complex strategy to resolve. People were compensated to overcome this challenge. Once the challenge was gone and the new way of doing business was a habit, the compensation reward structure didn't change. Be careful not to reward people for doing what's easy or routine. Continuously expect improved performance, always lifting the bar beyond routine.

> Be careful not to reward people for doing what's easy or routine. Continuously expect improved performance, always lifting the bar beyond routine.

Motivate your team according to the metrics you are monitoring. You are measuring it because you agreed it was important. If it's important, reward when goals are met or exceeded. Keep it simple. The key to metrics and using metrics to enhance employee engagement and business success is your team's ability to understand the connection between the measurement of the KPI and their enjoyment of success.

"Differing weights and differing measures—the Lord detests them both,"

Proverbs 20:10.

Chapter 5
Model Excellence

> *Commit to* **MODELING** *excellence.*
> *Complacency is the enemy of excellence*
> *and as a leader you'll never get*
> *better than you model or reward.*

Effectively motivating a team to deliver excellence is one of the biggest challenges leaders must overcome. The personal example that you set will have the biggest impact on your team's delivery of excellence than anything you say or any processes you implement. Our youngest daughter recently entered the restaurant service world. She was required to attend a food safety training class given at the corporate headquarters of her new employer. She learned the rules and procedures that she was expected to abide by as she undertook the duties of her job as a server. The rules required staff never to eat any food in the kitchen, as it was a violation of company policy and food handling safety rules.

After the educational training at corporate headquarters, she reported to the restaurant to learn the hands-on aspect of her job. Indeed, her trainer in the restaurant reinforced they were never to eat food in the kitchen. They could order food, but it was to be taken to a staff area of the dining room for consumption. However, on her very first day in the restaurant, and nearly every day thereafter, she witnessed otherwise. The general manager of the restaurant apparently really liked French fries. When the GM walked by the French fry bin where the prepared fries sat under a heat lamp, he would dip his hand in and take a few fries and eat them as he passed through the kitchen. In turn, our daughter saw nearly every restaurant staff person dip their hand in for fries and eat them as they walked by. Every member of the staff ate the French fries from the warming bin, in the kitchen, in violation of the rules. I asked her if the GM had given them verbal permission to break this "no eating in the kitchen" rule. She indicated he hadn't actually said anything about eating the French fries. She also said, "If corporate is around, I don't think anyone would do that, even him." The worst behavior the

> The worst behavior the leader models or allows is the best behavior the leader should expect from his or her team.

leader models or allows is the best behavior the leader should expect from his or her team.

Your behavior and performance sets the bar for those around you. Your words regarding your expectations of excellence actually have the lowest impact on the performance of others. What you do, what you overlook, and what you reward tells your team what is important to you. It's human nature that we know doing our best is a good and lauded thing. It's also human nature that if our best isn't recognized or even expected, and half our best gets the same response as those who give their all, we come to understand that "good enough" is … well … good enough. We'll deliver half of our best more often than not if excellence doesn't garner a different reaction. If our leader takes a shortcut, why would we ever follow all the rules when the shortcut is easier, quicker, and the behavior modeled by our leader.

> What you do, what you overlook, and what you reward tells your team what is important to you.

Excellence separates the average from those who are the best. Excellence requires us to work harder, be smarter, and think differently. Excellence is doing the extra thing and going the extra mile. If a customer asks for one thing, it's giving the customer that thing plus more and surprising them with the extra effort. As a leader, it's your job to inspire the efforts to achieve excellence in everything your team does, and to strive to accomplish more than is expected. If you don't model excellence, don't expect your team to deliver it.

> If you don't model excellence, don't expect your team to deliver it.

If mediocrity has been the status quo for your organization, delivering excellence may be a foreign concept to the team. The term is overused and generic in some settings, like an "excellent musical performance" or an "excellent meal". Used as an adjective to describe a product that is heads above the rest, excellence means the best, without flaw. Defining excellence in the delivery of our work is a less common use of the word. Excellence is something that as consumers we desire, but as producers few are able to deliver. You must inspire people to produce for reasons far beyond collecting a paycheck. "Excellence" is a difficult word to define. We all know when we see it or experience it, and we all know when it's missing. Still, it isn't easily reduced to a few bullet points. Rather, it's a feeling, a desire, a willingness to give better, do more, think smarter for the benefit of the greater good. It's a willingness to prepare better, practice more, rewrite the memo, analyze the numbers one more time, and to deliver the best. Excellence means going the extra mile every single time.

Team members will follow your example to aspire to excellence so long as you model the behavior and reward and recognize the efforts. Every day is a new day for you to lead your team to make their mark and to do it better than it's ever been done before. Encourage and praise those extra efforts to be excellent. When you strive for excellence, you'll surpass everyone else who doesn't, and you'll model the expectation for your team, who in turn will strive for excellence and surpass all others. Likewise, when you cut corners or allow less that excellent performance, you're sending a powerful message that good enough is good enough.

Complacency is the enemy of excellence. While consulting with a variety of different medical providers, I was hired by a physician practice to assist the team to prepare for a regulatory survey. I enjoyed this assignment because the team was technically competent and the leadership of the organization supported running the business in the right way. They desired to deliver excellence and were willing to spend money on necessary resources to support that goal.

As I observed the physical plant of the surgery center, I found it to be aging but in pretty good shape. I noticed several of the counter surfaces in each care area had cracks and chips in the Formica. I asked staff if they knew the cracks were there, and if they knew regulators would consider the cracks an infection control risk. Every staff member I asked indicated the cracks had been present for quite some time and that they knew them to be a potential risk where bacteria could set up house in the surface cracks. I then asked the team's leader if he knew about the aging Formica.

> Complacency is the enemy of excellence.

He indicated he did, but he just hadn't made it a priority to fix. He knew it would be a negative observation to regulatory surveyors. He had the budgeted dollars to fix it, everyone knew it needed to be fixed, but it just wasn't his priority. The practice had a solid infection control plan in place with several elements that I would say exceeded industry standard, yet there was a tangible example that keeping the physical environment up to infection control standards wasn't deemed important. Could we really expect teammates to exceed industry standards and strive for excellence in the area of infection control when there was such a tangible, obvious example of complacency in the very area they sought to exceed?

> What you ignore, your team will ignore. The worst behavior or output that you are willing to tolerate is the best you can expect from your team.

In another workplace, I was given a spreadsheet of numbers that the team told me they reviewed daily to determine their progress. One column of numbers didn't make sense to me, so I asked team members to explain the numbers. Each one, including the team leader, indicated to me those numbers weren't correct, as the data pulled to calculate the formula came from a source that wasn't reliable. As a result, they simply ignored that column of the report. The team worked to deliver a daily report that they all knew had information in it that was inaccurate. I surmised that the report wasn't actually meaningful to the team, nor did it hold a lot of weight. When I interviewed staff, I discovered most never even looked at the report at all, because they didn't see it as an accurate indicator of their performance. The leader confessed he actually never looked at that report. But it took an hour a day for the team to generate it.

What you ignore, your team will ignore. The worst behavior or output that you are willing to tolerate is the best you can expect from your team. The leader who set the bar high in nine out of ten areas but didn't care about the tenth shouldn't expect excellence in any area. The leader who distributed a daily report with a faulty calculation was sending the message that accuracy didn't matter as long as you got the report out on time, and as a result encouraged the team to ignore what they knew wasn't right. And in the restaurant where our daughter worked, the GM's actions told an entire staff of food workers that a rule doesn't matter if the boss doesn't think it matters, or when corporate isn't looking. These leaders were all competent in their roles, but all were complacent and, without intending it, modeled mediocrity instead of excellence. Complacency is the enemy of excellence. You simply can't expect others to produce more than you yourself are willing to do.

Think about what excellence in your workplace should look like. Then model it, teach it, and reward it. The work product is always the

> Think about what excellence in your workplace should look like. Then model it, teach it, and reward it.

result of the effort spent in creating the result. If every task is modeled in excellence, there can be only one kind of result—excellence. Reduce this term to defined behaviors in your work setting. For example, in a call center, it may include speaking a required script with a smile on your face (which translates to kindness to the customer).[2]

In marketing, it may mean taking time to get the colors in the creative exactly right. In customer service, it might mean listening carefully and delivering the extra benefit that the customer hoped for but didn't ask for. Think about the production responsibilities of your team and define what excellence looks like. Ask your teammates. They know what excellence throughout their workflow should look like, and where it's lacking. Then work together to identify areas where process improvement will ensure excellent results.

> If you overlook behavior that is inconsistent with the company's values, don't expect your team to believe that the company values are real.

You'll never get better from your team than the bar you set. This may be one of the hardest lessons to learn as a new leader, and one of the hardest to turn around if you get it wrong. It's a challenge to balance

---

2   "Smile—And The World Can Hear You, Even If You Hide," ScienceDaily. Accessed August 16, 2016, https://www.sciencedaily.com/releases/2008/01/080111224745.htm.

between setting boundaries and rules for the team, and creating an environment and culture that recognizes team members where they are. Precedent matters. What you value, your team will value. And what you don't value will be obvious to everyone around you. If you constantly begin meetings ten minutes late and have little regard for the scheduled end time, you can't expect better than that from your team. If you expect 80 percent accuracy rate on a metric for which your team is measured, don't expect the team to deliver 90 percent. If you don't follow the company dress code, don't expect others to value it. If you overlook behavior that is inconsistent with the company's values, don't expect your team to believe that the company values are real.

This is especially difficult if you're promoted from the ranks and now manage people in positions that you once held. You have a keen understanding of the pressures they hold in their positions and the barriers that exist for them that may actually be inhibiting excellent performance. You may be tempted to change expectations and cut them some slack for non-performance. Don't. If the expectations or KPIs set for your team aren't reasonable, that's one thing. It's your job as the leader to ensure that you are letting the folks above you understand the challenges that exist. Failing to hold your team accountable to excellence won't increase performance or inspire out of the box thinking to overcome challenges or improve processes.

I remember as a young nursing student a lesson that stuck with me from a hospital clinical instructor. Walking down the hallway with our group, she stopped to pick up a piece of garbage that was dropped on the floor. She simply said, "If you walk by garbage, you're indicating to everyone that you think it's appropriate that garbage is thrown on the hospital floor, and it's ok to throw more there." That instructor was teaching excellence. To this day you won't find me walking by garbage, whether it's in a work hallway or some other venue. To walk by it would indicate that I somehow condone the sloppy behavior of throwing garbage on the floor.

One team I inherited had been previously managed by a leader with a very dictatorial style. Performance had historically been rewarded solely on output and KPIs, with little to no regard for integrity or teamwork. I let the team know moving forward that excellence would be expected and rewarded. Performance without regard for the values of integrity and care would no longer be recognized as success. The change in leadership focus was mostly widely embraced; however a few of those top KPI performers weren't impressed. They were accustomed to being rewarded for output without regard for their lack of respect for integrity and teamwork. When they didn't respond to efforts to coach to improvement, I fired them. The "best" at delivering KPIs were fired. Making a tough decision and letting a few of the top performers go sent a loud message. I would only accept the best output if it was delivered with the highest regard for the company's values with excellence. I never had to send a message like that again. The rest of the team understood that value adherence plus performance output would equal success.

Excellence isn't perfection. But it is perfect effort. As a leader you must inspire teammates to desire to deliver excellence. Think of yourself as a conductor. Every member of your team must work in proper cadence with the other members of their section, and each section in proper cadence with the others. If every member has done their best, given their highest effort, and practiced, practiced, practiced, the result will be an excellent performance.

> You're not always going to get it right, and exhibiting honesty and humility when you get it wrong will go a long way to keeping the team motivated and inspired.

Finally, you're human. Some days you aren't going to feel like being excellent. When you mess up and the stress of the day gets the better of you, or you overlook a shortcut from a teammate, stop and correct the deviation immediately. Honestly communicate what happened, why you changed the standards even momentarily, apologize, reinforce the expectation moving forward, and move forward to another day. You're not always going to get it right, and exhibiting honesty and humility when you get it wrong will go a long way to keeping the team motivated and inspired. When striving for excellence, it's important that you don't overlook failures that will happen. Admit mistakes, model what right looks like, and move on.

Consider the long-term impact of your stamp of approval on mediocrity. You may think in the moment that you're helping your team by allowing a corner to be cut. Resist. It will be difficult to get that corner back. Somewhere deep inside even the most resistant follower has a desire to make a difference—and be the best at what they do. Appeal to that inner gold medal winner and inspire people to be their best. Excellence is a key ingredient in the secret sauce of leading well.

> "Do you see someone skilled in their work? They will serve before kings; they will not serve before officials of low rank,"
>
> Proverbs 22:29.

Chapter 6
Honor Others

> *People are the most important asset of your organization.*
> **COMMIT** *to honor them in the good times and the bad.*

One small team I led had a monthly tradition still remembered fondly by its members. We would gather during lunch, each bringing a dish to share. One of us was tasked with "leading" the lunch by telling the group something about ourselves that the others didn't know. That was the only instruction (besides, of course, keeping the content appropriate). We could literally talk about anything when it was our turn to lead. One woman brought in a video of herself in a punk rock band from decades earlier. We watched that video, seeing her decades-younger self as the lead singer with rocker hair. We laughed together until we cried. You can imagine the bonding that occurred during that activity when we shared personal and potentially embarrassing details like that with each other. It filled out our understanding of each other as people, not just as professionals in a role. It bonded us together and unified our efforts. The care we shared for each other was genuine and lasted years beyond our working relationship ended when that particular business was sold.

> Think of your people more, and yourself less. Honoring others is a key ingredient in the secret sauce.

Perhaps C.S. Lewis said it best, "True humility is not thinking less of yourself; it is thinking of yourself less."[3] A humble heart is one of the most charismatic qualities any leader can possess. The characteristic of humility is a powerful witness to those you lead, showing you value them and their needs above your own. Humility is more than kind words. Humility is a verb—it requires action to prove it. Sacrificing your time, attention, and even economic gain for the benefit of others are all tangible ways of measuring a humble heart. Pride in oneself is the enemy of humility. If you think you're "all that," this may be an area you want to work on as a leader. Think of your people more,

---

3   C.S. Lewis, *Mere Christianity* (New York: MacMillan Publishing Company, 1952),

The Secret Sauce

and yourself less. Honoring others is a key ingredient in the secret sauce.

As a new leader at the beginning of my career many years ago, I was focused on improving patient care in the hospital unit I was responsible for. It was clear to me where the missteps were and what processes needed to be changed in order to end up with improved patient care and patient satisfaction. New in my role of managing people, and new to a position of authority that gave me the power to simply change procedures at my command, I started yielding orders. Some lessons we learn the hard way, but they're valuable nonetheless.

> As you honor others, sacrificially look out for the interests of those you lead above your own interests. A willingness to put your own skin in the game is one of the best ways to lead well, and to earn respect and loyalty from your team.

As I was handing out the orders to an already overloaded nursing staff, one young, smart-mouthed nurse told me that if I spent some time understanding my employees' workload and challenges before piling on more responsibilities, they'd feel valued and like their jobs more. In turn, she said, they'd be better able to take better care of our patients.

This rambunctious young woman never had the opportunity to know how she would impact my leadership thinking, because she walked out of the job that day. She'd never get to know that I took her angry words to heart. While her delivery wasn't quite right, her message rang true. Take care of your employees, and they'll take care of your customers. The lesson of humility was hidden in her angry words. I needed first to understand why the team was falling short, and take the time to hear their concerns. Then together we could work to strategize process improvements when they understood that I knew their plight.

As you honor others, sacrificially look out for the interests of those you lead above your own interests. A willingness to put your own skin in the game is one of the best ways to lead well, and to earn respect and loyalty from your team. Great leaders put the needs of others above their own in tangible ways. The team in turn responds to these acts in remarkable ways. These acts can be big or small. Essentially, your actions show your team that you're not asking them to do something that you aren't willing to do. This can be as simple as ensuring that if you are expecting people to work hours that are inconvenient, you show your support by being present during those inconvenient hours.

For example, if your workplace has around the clock shifts, and your team is responsible for shifts around the clock, you sacrifice and show up on each shift to provide support and leadership from time to time. Imagine the impact of showing up at 3:00 a.m. with a treat and taking time for an impromptu staff meeting with your night shift. That will get attention. What if you gave up your office for a cubicle and instead converted the office to team meeting space? What if you gave up your personalized parking space for a performer of the month? What if you never allowed your team's bonuses to be held unless you held your own? Putting your people first requires sacrifice. You can't put your people first if you're always thinking of your own gain.

How well do you know what's important to your teammates? What is your team's top performer's significant other's name? What about the names of that person's children? What does this person aspire to do in the future professionally? Where did he or she go to school? What is their degree in? Now think of your least successful teammate. Ask yourself the same questions. Do you know the answers in each case? How well do you know the members of your team? While some might tell you work is their passion, most people you meet in the workplace will tell you they are working to financially support their life. Motivating them and inspiring their best will require you to know something about their dreams and aspirations and to honor those in tangible ways. Know what your teammates consider to be their "life." Get to know what is important to your team members and let them know those things are important to you as well.

One gentleman I managed invented a product that was unique and special and that had the potential to significantly improve the world of tattoo art. This hobby had nothing to do with our company or his day job. It was his passion and extremely important to him, and he would speak of it from time to time.

I made a point of spending a few minutes online one night in order to educate myself on the world of tattoo art so that I could understand what he was dreaming of accomplishing. I then could have intelligent conversations with him about this passion, and check in from time to time on his progress. My interest and small investment of time showed him I valued him as more than a competent asset to my team (he was in fact one of the most valuable teammates I've ever had the honor to lead). I valued him as a professional, but I also valued him as a person with dreams and aspirations outside of our workplace.

Whenever possible, meet your people where they are. Have a spirit of care and compassion concerning them. You are leading a team to deliver KPIs and business goals, and collectively the group is focused on business initiatives. The more you recognize that your team is made up of individuals with hopes, dreams, and goals, you'll find yourself better equipped to help them deliver their best collectively while reaching for their individual dreams as well. Some of your teammates will be top performers with a focus on promotion and forward movement in your company. Others will be struggling with personal crisis, like a loved one battling cancer or a disabled child at home. Whatever their story, every human being has one, and great leaders meet their people where they are, encouraging them to rise above their circumstances.

We all need to accomplish our job duties and deliver results, but only leaders who recognize that each individual comes with his or her own challenges to the job will garner the loyalty and drive that dedicated team members possess. Whenever possible, think out of the box to help your team members succeed. For the top performer who wants to be promoted, create a formal mentoring program. For the average performer who is caring for an elderly parent at home, problem solve potential flexible work opportunities. You'll often find that's all it takes for that average performer to become a top performer—understanding what's holding them back.

> The more you recognize that your team is made up of individuals with hopes, dreams, and goals, you'll find yourself better equipped to help them deliver their best collectively, while reaching for their individual dreams as well.

There are a few simple things you can do to show people you care. Listen to their stories and remember their family members' names. Call people by their given name when you interact with them. The national institute of health published a study on the positive impact in the brain when human beings hear their first name used.[4] Every time. Nicknames are fun, but science shows that when we hear our given names, we are motivated to perform in ways superior

---

[4] "Brain Activation When Hearing One's Own and Others' Names," US National Library of Medicine, accessed August 16, 2016, http://www.ncbi.nlm.nih.gov/pmc/articles/PMC1647299/.

than when we don't hear our name. In the workplace, when you take the time to learn, remember, and then use teammates' first names, you're sending a message to them that they are valuable, unique, and important to you.

Honor people by listening to their ideas. Create forums and environments in which teammates know their thoughts and creativity are appreciated and welcomed. Your teammates have great insights into improving the workplace and how to successfully meet and exceed goals. A humble leader listens and adopts great ideas from teammates, which in turn fosters more creative thinking. Don't be afraid to ask for ideas. Your willingness to be vulnerable and admit you are waiting for the right solution will make you a stronger leader to your team.

> "Be devoted to one another in love. Honor one another above yourselves,"
>
> Romans 12:10.

Chapter 7
Praise and Recognize

> *Commit to offering genuine* **PRAISE** *and recognition for a job well done.*

Everyone appreciates encouragement and responds to honest positive reinforcement. Every member of your team is waiting for you to understand and recognize his or her contributions to the success of the organization. They're also watching for your reaction to other teammates' contributions and measuring your competency, authenticity, and character by their perceived accuracy of the praise and recognition that you deliver.

As human beings, we have an innate need to understand how we fit into the bigger picture, and to believe that we matter and that our efforts are noticed. We

> Most people want to be successful in the workplace. Most get up every single day, get dressed, and head to work with the intention of completing their job assignments well.

desire to be individually acknowledged for our contributions, skills, and competency. Talk to people around you who seem to just be going through the motions in their job or who are outright dissatisfied with their workplace and ask them why they are so unhappy. Most will tell you they just aren't appreciated for what they do. No one notices their contributions, and no one recognizes their hard work and dedication. It's equally predictable that these employees are simply punching the clock and doing their job until something better comes along. We all know people who feel this way about their workplace. In general, they are so dissatisfied that they can be miserable to be around. Maybe you've even felt this way yourself from time to time.

Most people want to be successful in the workplace. Most get up every single day, get dressed, and head to work with the intention of completing their job assignments well. That doesn't mean they will meet that goal, but they start out each day with the right desires. Unfortunately, there are always people who don't actually care about doing a good job. You'll need to weed those people out. If your team genuinely desires to do well, that's a great foundation upon which to build. In other words, look at your team as a group of individuals with individual capabilities and drive, who each desire to do well and who each want to be satisfied in their jobs. Each day is a new day to lead this team to a better place.

Praise is key for showing appreciation. It should take the form of private and public encouragement and should be specific in nature to increase credibility. Praise and recognition is key to building employee engagement and should be given frequently. In order to effectively encourage your team members, you need to ensure that you know what each person is responsible for, and what each person actually does. That seems obvious, but depending on the size of your team and where you find yourself in the organization, you may lead many different types of competencies and skill sets. As a result, you may not know the actual nuts and bolts of each job. Because recognition needs to be genuine, if you don't really know what someone is supposed to be accomplishing, it will be difficult to measure his or her success and recognize it accurately. This can easily be remedied. Take time to spend time with each member of your team.

If you are a new leader, make one-on-one meetings your first priority in your role. If your work environment allows, shadow your team members for a period of time.

> If you are a new leader, make one-on-one meetings your first priority in your role. If your work environment allows, shadow your team members for a period of time.

It's very important that you let each person know that you want a deeper understanding of his or her responsibilities. Be humble as you set up these meetings. If this isn't a common part of your organization's culture, people might think you're watching them for some punitive purpose. It's very important that you let your team know that you want a clear understanding of what they are responsible for and how you can help them be successful. While you are shadowing, ask the teammates for their insights regarding what parts of their job seem to them to be time-wasters or inefficiencies. After all, no one knows where the inefficient processes are better than the people closest to those steps in the inefficient process. Your purpose is to come away from the experience with a better understanding of the team member's job so that you can lead them more effectively towards success.

Even if you have been promoted from the ranks that you are now managing, this is still an important step. You may think you know your former peers' job responsibilities and performances well. Some of them may have desired to get the promotion you just received. This is a great opportunity for you to show humility and use the same technique to learn your team members' roles, even if you think you should already know them. Be humble, allow frank,

> In order to deliver genuine feedback and recognition, you need to show your team that you care about what they do and understand how they do it.

honest communication, and you'll walk away with different information and a better understanding about the roles of your team members than you had when you were their peer. Taking time to listen and observe is an important step in recognizing each team member for his or her individual contributions and needs. It will also give those who were passed over for the promotion an opportunity to communicate to you their value, as they'll likely tell you why they thought they were ready for the job.

Taking the time to get a comprehensive foundation of knowledge about your team's duties will be a meaningful exercise. In order to deliver genuine feedback and recognition, you need to show your team that you care about what they do and understand how they do it. In the process of encouraging your team, you're building your own value to your team. You actually are learning how you can make a difference to the team's success. If you aren't able to shadow team members, or if you lead too many people to make this a practical approach, then set up individual or group meetings to discuss job duties. Your role in these meetings is to listen. Set the expectation that you desire to understand what is expected of each member of your team, and that you want to hear his or her perspectives and ideas.

Now that you know what each person on your team is responsible for, you can accurately and effectively measure their success in carrying out these duties. This is where you'll begin recognizing each person for his or her individual and team contributions. You've also picked up some valuable information regarding process improvement needs, but set those aside for now. Encouragement builds confidence and team engagement. A team that feels valued will be more likely to work together to solve those very inefficiencies you've discovered, and together they'll improve processes.

In meetings, or when walking around your team area, give specific positive feedback in order to motivate the team and elevate your credibility as a leader that knows what's going on. For example, "You're doing a great job" without specificity won't deliver nearly the same encouragement as, "You really did a tremendous job with the work you did on Mr. Jones' account. I really appreciate your extra effort to meet with him personally!" Being specific with praise and recognition shows you care enough to recognize individual accomplishments.

Ensure your use of public praise is fair, genuine, and meaningful. If someone on your team is particularly worthy, then let that person know that's how you see him or her. Don't be afraid to say you count on their performance to make the entire team better. Specific examples encourage team members to continue driving with those qualities that are really making a difference. Your goal is to highlight and enhance the genuine value of each team member. Consider employing opportunities for team members to recognize each other as well. During weekly team meetings, ask for team members to recognize the contributions of others. These public opportunities are always for the delivery of recognition and praise for the purpose of building up the team. Remember, constructive criticism is always delivered privately.

Keep encouragement up to date. If you can't comment positively on things your team is currently working on, this will tell you it's time for you to take a step back and ask questions, talk, and observe. I worked with one leader who loved to provide encouragement. Unfortunately, he was caught in a time warp. He would give the same public recognition to the same group of people time after time after time. He never updated his list of employees whom he believed deserved praise, nor could he speak about those teammates' current contribution. As a result, the encouragement not only was worthless to the team, but it highlighted his lack of connection and diminished his leadership value to the team.

> Use personal hand-written notes to encourage your team.

We live in an electronic world where most communication at work happens via computer utilizing email or chat. While these are efficient methods they're not very personal. Use personal hand-written notes to encourage your team. If someone makes a particular contribution that is significant, send a hand written card of thanks to his or her home. There is nothing quite like coming home after a challenging day at work to find a note of encouragement in the mailbox that even allows your family to see what a difference you're making. Taking the time to personalize praise and recognition, directing it to specific accomplishments or qualities, and taking time to deliver it in a manner that shows you dedicate time to it, will increase its value to the recipient.

> You want to be so proficient that when you speak words of encouragement, they are known to be true and an accurate measure of performance.

When you encourage people and recognize their contributions, you lift their spirits and motivate them. There is nothing quite as encouraging as walking through your team area and seeing your notes of encouragement hanging on work stations for all to see. People need encouragement; they hold these edifying words close to them. You in turn get the satisfaction of knowing the time you're taking to recognize and encourage is lifting others up, boosting their self-confidence, and improving their performance. Mix it up and stay creative in your delivery. You want to be so proficient that when you speak words of encouragement, they are known to be true and an accurate measure of performance.

Many companies have employee recognition programs, and I learned a lot about fellow leaders on the team when our company program was implemented. Every quarter, it was the manager's job to nominate members of their team for recognition. Final selections were made by a selection committee, but teammates could only get "on the list" for selection if nominated by their manager. I remember one department leader in particular. Every quarter without exception she would nominate nearly every member of her team for an award. She would supply detailed lists of the accomplishments of each teammate for the quarter, and she would strongly advocate for each to win an award. I can't remember a quarter when this team didn't have at least one winner selected by the committee. She was well respected and had nearly zero staff turnover. Her team delivered exceptional results, and it wasn't unusual for them to not only meet but also exceed monthly goals. Recognizing great performance was important to her, and it showed in the culture of the department and the results from the team.

> Encouragement should always be genuine in its delivery and honest in its assessment.

In contrast, there were a few managers who didn't submit any nominations. They would cite the process was too time consuming. In some cases, the managers even indicated none of their teammates were award-worthy. Not surprisingly, these teams had higher turnover and lower production. The participation in the quarterly awards process was an excellent barometer of leading well. Great leaders care about nurturing, growing, recognizing, and rewarding their team. If they didn't feel like the recognition was worth the time or warranted by the team, it was highly unlikely those leaders were serving their teams well to ensure success.

If your company has a formal employee recognition program, make certain you know how it works and how

> The flip side of praise and recognition is holding underperformers accountable.

to access it. Your team members will appreciate these formal opportunities for recognition, as well as the informal ones discussed above. If your company doesn't have a formal employee recognition program, don't hesitate to create one for use with your team. One team I knew that was especially positively engaged chose to award a huge wrestling belt to the employee whose performance had the most impact on the team hitting its monthly KPIs. Each month, the team would meet briefly in a common area, share KPI results, and cheer loudly as the belt was passed on to the newest recipient. Everyone received a shout out during this meeting for individual milestones, but receiving the coveted belt was met with great enthusiasm and high-fiving. Everyone wanted to win the belt, and the day-to-day environment of encouraging performance promoted friendly competition and teamwork.

Offering someone praise and encouragement and positive reinforcement should not be employed simply because it's a sound business strategy. Encouragement should always be genuine in its delivery and honest in its assessment. Don't walk around telling everyone they're working hard and doing a good job. That form of praise will be meaningless cheerleading. In contrast, offering genuine, authentic, intentional, specific praise and encouragement is a powerful way to validate the person's self-worth. You're inspiring people to perform well. Take the time to recognize them when they do.

Your authenticity in praise will also give you greater authority when addressing areas where your team members need to improve. The flip side of praise and recognition is holding under-performers accountable. One leader I worked with had a special knack for delivering encouragement. She was tough but fair. The team could count on her to recognize their individual and group achievements in consistent and authentic ways. She would write notes of encouragement, or walk through work areas and provide verbal words of affirmation. Just as important, the team could count on her to recognize when a teammate's performance was falling behind expectations. She knew the performance of her team because she was engaged and communicated the status of KPIs routinely. Everyone knew where the team stood from a performance perspective globally. She would then work one on one to improve performance with teammates who fell behind. She would set expectations privately, collaborate with them to improve shortcomings, help them set their course, and hold them accountable if improvements didn't follow. She never let under performers hold back the overall performance of the team. People will only continue to drive exceptional results when they know they are appreciated for their high performance. Don't coddle, protect, or overlook poor performance. To do so eliminates the trust you've built, and your words

> Your authenticity in praise will also give you greater authority when addressing areas where your team members need to improve.

of affirmation become meaningless if you won't also have the difficult conversations.

Praise and recognition are effective motivators when delivered honestly with authenticity and up-to-date knowledge of performance. It is a key driver of employee satisfaction and loyalty on your team. Be a leader who drives performance by recognizing those who go above and beyond for the company. Don't leave anyone out. Teammates are either worthy of some type of praise, or you should be having private conversations about performance improvement.

Make certain you don't play favorites and only notice the performers at the end of the KPI chain. For example, those who ultimately obtain the sales often receive sales awards. But there are many people along the sales chain in less visible jobs who may be equally deserving of praise for the end result. The creative associate who helped develop the marketing collateral may well have played an important role in the success of the salesperson who closed the sale. Don't forget departmental assistants who carry a big load but often don't receive the recognition they deserve for holding the entire department together. In healthcare, doctors often get recognized, but I can tell you it is often the assistant who makes or breaks the effectiveness of the physician by keeping her schedule organized, and the doctor heading in the right direction.

The Secret Sauce

If you manage other leaders, make certain to also take time to recognize their efforts to lead well. Measure the performance and leadership effectiveness of the leaders you manage by holding "skip level" meetings. At scheduled intervals, meet with teammates who report to leaders who directly report to you. These skip level meetings can be held in individual or group settings. Keep the meetings conversational and informal, and always let your direct reports know they are taking place. Keep a loose agenda, get a feel for what the teammates like about their jobs, what they wish was different, and what barriers they perceive to their success. Listen to what they're telling you. The impact of the leader's style on the team will be easily evident in how they discuss their work. These meetings will give you insights into not only the leaders who report to you, but also into the culture that you are building within your organization. If you are leading well, then leaders under you will follow your model and lead well, too. The team will come to depend upon this open forum to get information directly to you. They'll also use it to offer praise and support for people they believe are top performers. After these meetings, use the feedback you've received to coach, teach, train, as well as offer praise and recognition for the positive things you've learned about the leader as part of this exercise. Skip level meetings are a great way to motivate and inspire the team. Providing open forums for communication, frequent praise, encouragement to motivate, honest feedback, and private correction will result in highly motivated teammates driving exceptional results.

"Therefore encourage one another and build each other up, just as in fact you are doing,"

1 Thessalonians 5:11.

Chapter 8
Communicate Often and Honestly

> *Commit to being* **ACCESSIBLE**, *intentional, and predictable with communication.*

One manager I know led a group of IT personnel. This particular team was a very tech savvy group of folks who worked diligently and were very focused on computer program development. They didn't interact with each other after hours, and they weren't particularly openly relational at work. Because of their introverted personalities, they could have easily been labeled as people who didn't care about what was going on around them. Nothing could be further from the truth. These were some of the smartest teammates in the company, and the quality of their program design depended upon their knowledge of the company's operations. They needed access to information and frequent communications regarding the business and its future plans. Because they were introverts, they didn't want the communication to come in the form of team meetings and one-on-ones. Instead, they used a chat application as a forum to open dialogue to gather operations information, learn about business initiatives, develop strategic plans, and communicate their development progress. This team was very comfortable with the chat environment. Questions and answers went back and forth throughout the day. The team felt included, empowered, and knowledgeable, and their performance and productivity reflected the same.

> Before words even begin to flow, certain expectations and perceived norms exist that will impact how your message is interpreted and received.

Everyone wants information. People want to know what you expect of them and why. People want to understand long and short term plans of the organization. They want to know where any organization is going, how the organization intends to get there, how the performance of the team fits into those broader organizational goals, and how they personally fit into any of that. People want to know that their future is secure, and that they are building their own future while they participate in the success of the organization. People simply want to know. The more they trust

The Secret Sauce

you, the more they'll trust that you'll tell them what's important to them when it's important for them to know it.

Communicate honestly. We live in a transparent world where information is readily available at the touch of our Google machine. Information is readily available in abundance and in an easy- to-digest format in all aspects of our lives. Expect your team to gauge how well you understand the business and how much they can trust you in part by how effectively you communicate relevant information to them. People bring experiences and beliefs into every conversation. Before words even begin to flow, certain expectations and perceived norms exist that will impact how your message is interpreted and received. It's important that you have a good understanding of these expectations so that communications are delivered effectively.

> Expect your team to gauge how well you understand the business and how much they can trust you in part by how effectively you communicate relevant information to them.

If you can't communicate honestly, don't communicate. People don't want to be lied to, and if you do lie, you'll lose the trust you've built. Some leaders don't trust the culture of a team to absorb bad news. Instead of delivering unpopular decisions or unfavorable results, these leaders create stories to manipulate the reaction of the team. While this may result in short term motivation, you can't continue to motivate a team with lies. The truth will at some point reveal itself, and you will lose the respect and trust of the team. If there is a business reason you can't communicate truthfully, you need to be honest about that as well. This may include letting the team know that there are proprietary reasons that you can't provide additional information, but that you need them to follow your lead and deliver results. Provide assurance and direction. If you've effectively built your trust account, your team will trust you and respect that you aren't making up lies to motivate them.

> Create predictable routine methods that you'll use to communicate information to your team and then ensure you stick with it.

Communication is a tool that should be used to make the team stronger. The strength of your trust account will determine how and when you need to communicate. Serving them, hiring well, mentoring, praising them—all the concepts we've already discussed builds team trust in your leadership. Create predictable routine methods that you'll use to communicate information to your team and then ensure you stick with it. Over time, the team will expect these avenues to deliver honest feedback regarding company performance, future plans, and organizational improvement strategies.

How effectively leaders in an organization communicate tells much about the culture of the company. Some leaders view information as power to be held close to the chest, and they don't share with the team for fear it will weaken their authority. If you want to gauge the culture of any organization, look at the exchange of information within. The quality, credibility, frequency, predictability, and the detail and forum in which information is presented will directly correspond to the engagement and trust of the team. The tone and tenor will also tell you a lot about the character and strength of the leadership delivering the communication.

You don't have to be at the top of an organization to share information. While you do have to honor the rules of those above you, share with your team the things that you are allowed to share. If there are important details you can't share, communicate that to your team as well. Silence or lack of communication breeds distrust, so even knowing that you are working on something you can't discuss but that will prove to be very exciting in the future will help to build that foundation of trust.

How often and by what means you share information to your team will become the infrastructure of the culture of your team. Identify what communication avenues exist for your team, both formal and informal. Formal methods might include team meetings, weekly emails, and one on one meetings. Informal communication might include chatter in the lunchroom or at the water cooler, social media, and the rumor mill. Harnessing the power of both formal and informal communication venues will be key to your team's exceptional performance.

Communication goes both ways. Ensure opportunities exist for teammates to communicate openly and honestly up the ladder as well as receiving information from you. The chat application in the IT team example worked well because the informal environment that included one leader and numerous teammates was a familiar, safe environment in which teammates could ask questions and gain encouragement for each other as they sought to share ideas, suggest innovations and business solutions, and even hash out new strategies. Think outside the box and consider your listener's capabilities, needs, and desires when creating open avenues for them to send (and for you to receive) important ideas and information. Think about how your teammates communicate with each other, and you will have identified a good forum for them to communicate with you.

Be predictable with information sharing. If you set expectations and a pattern of honest information exchange, your team will settle in to trust that schedule. They won't spend valuable time wondering what's going on between predictable communications. Instead, they'll trust that if there is something they need to know, you've either already told them, or you'll tell them at the time they need to know.

The Secret Sauce

"Like apples of gold in settings of silver is a ruling rightly given,"

Proverbs 25:11.

Chapter 9
Mentor and Invest

> *You are **UNIQUELY** situated to impact lives in significant ways every day. Whether you intend to or not, you're always mentoring others in your path.*

I've had the privilege of mentoring many teammates over the years. Some have had as great an impact on me as I've had on them. One woman, who I'll call Jamie, was assigned as part of a formal program to be mentored by me. Jamie changed how I view mentoring forever. Picking up new skills and competencies outside her core profession required hard work, and Jamie's efforts were impressive as she worked tirelessly to increase her scope of knowledge. She was a very eager learner. Ultimately, she was one of the most dedicated people I have ever mentored. The growth she exhibited as a result of the exercise would become the benchmark for every other mentee under my responsibility still today. She made herself available to take on new assignments, and worked hard to learn the things that didn't come easy to her.

Jamie was assigned to me as part of a formal three-month mentoring program. She had applied for the assignment and had been selected as part of a competitive process. She was a subject matter expert in her own field, but had little to no management experience or business training. The purpose of our relationship was for her to grow in these areas of expertise. Jamie was a physician assistant and I was leading a large national healthcare practice. It definitely took time at the beginning of our relationship for her to understand that in order to run a successful organization, she would need to understand that there was a complex business operation that had nothing to do with practicing medicine that she would need to learn and understand. We met formally for an hour once a week. I also chose to give her access to my calendar so that she could join any meeting that her schedule allowed her to, so long as the subjects of the meeting agreed. Jamie quickly learned by sitting through these meetings that there was much she didn't know or understand about running practice operations. That didn't surprise me. What did surprise me was what she did with that newfound understanding.

The Secret Sauce

At our weekly meetings, Jamie would come prepared with a summary of each additional meeting she had attended that week. She would first let me know what her impressions were regarding what the meeting was about. Often, especially if the meeting was financial in nature, she'd indicate she had been lost. But she took copious notes, and after the meeting—and usually at home after her shift—Jamie would get on the Internet and research terminology she'd heard in the meeting that she didn't understand. She would research the concepts and subject matter of the meetings. Then when she'd already put in more effort than I expected her to, she would present suggestions to me regarding where she thought we should go next in that process. Sometimes the plan was already in motion, so she was looking for confirmation that she was on the right track. But other times her exercise of research and strategizing actually produced an idea that the team hadn't considered yet. She was committed to learning everything she could during our formal period of mentoring, and the effort she committed to being successful was impressive.

When Jamie's three months were up, I missed her. Her commitment, curiosity, stamina, drive, and tenacity had impacted me as much as it benefitted her. She left the program wiser and ready for promotion. Because she exhausted every opportunity given to her as part

> Share your experiences and life lessons as you teach, encourage, and lift up others around you.

of the program, her scope of influence had widened substantially. As my mentee, while competently completing her own job, she made my job easier and enhanced the effectiveness of the team. Additionally, formal mentoring would forevermore be compared to how Jamie experienced the program. She set the bar for all future mentees. Jamie reminded me that being mentored, as well as mentoring, is a verb. After Jamie, I never accepted a mentee into a formal mentoring program who didn't understand that the relationship would take hard work, dedication, and a huge dose of self-drive for the individual to learn and be successful. I would tell them what a successful program engagement looked like, and I described Jamie's experience. And Jamie did even more than just change my mentoring. I ask more questions and research more for the sake of learning new concepts and competencies.

> People want what you have—your favor, your knowledge, your position, your abilities, and your insights.

People want what you have—your favor, your knowledge, your position, your abilities, and your insights. The time you spend giving of yourself to build up others will come back to you tenfold as people enthusiastically soak up the knowledge and the wisdom that you impart as your share your journey with others. If people aren't striving to be where you are, reflect on your leadership style to ensure you're practicing the ingredients we've explored in previous chapters. Share your

The Secret Sauce

experiences and life lessons as you teach, encourage, and lift up others around you.

You probably often think about people who have helped you get where you are today— those who've impacted your marketplace thinking, those from whose modeling you've learned, and those in whose footsteps you hope to walk. These are people who have influenced your career and who have helped to mold you into the leader you are today. Just as others have done for you, you have an important responsibility to be a person of influence to others whose lives you touch every day. Regardless of how old you are or how many years you've been in the working world, your positional perspective as a leader, your experiences, and your worldview give you the resources you need to help others reach their dreams and aspirations.

As you grow in management roles, you will have more opportunities to mentor people. Most will be the informal opportunities that arise each day. Learn to adopt a spirit of mentoring in everything you do. Strive to teach, train, pour into, and support those around you. Lead by example, and leave any workplace better because of the seeds you've planted along the way. Train up those around you who will do better things than you have done.

Once people recognize you as a teacher, don't be surprised when you are asked to enter into some sort of formal mentoring partnership. Mentoring relationships take time and commitment. You can't purposefully serve multiple people in a formal mentoring capacity at one time and do it well. I learned quickly that I needed to identify high potential teammates that I can effectively influence and meaningfully impact . And I had to ensure they shared certain personality traits that I respected. That way I would be as excited to invest in their journey as they were excited about the mentoring experience.

> Train up those around you who will do better things than you have done.

Mentoring takes time. It will be nearly impossible for you to mentor someone you don't like, or worse, don't respect. Know your own appetite for mentoring before you respond to these requests. For people who I didn't feel led to mentor, I would generally point them in the right direction to someone else who might be able to provide them with a meaningful mentoring arrangement. Mentoring should never be wasted time for either the teammate or the leader, so become comfortable saying no. The time spent should benefit both the mentor and the mentee. It is not unusual for me to have people approach me and ask if I will mentor them. I always ask them what they hope to gain from the relationship. If they can't articulate more than, "I want to learn from you," we don't proceed. I want to see genuine reflection when answering this question. The person should be able to articulate exactly what they hope to gain by the exchange. The mentee's desire should extend beyond their hope that interacting with you will be good for their career.

Have a standard process for mentoring others and stick to it. That will allow you to honor your own time, and theirs. This might include creating a formal outline to identify the rules for the mentoring relationship. Set milestones for the relationship and agree how success will be measured. Agree on a communication schedule and stick to it. Meetings can be live or by phone, but should be assigned a schedule to ensure accountability of both parties. If you desire to support the mentee outside of the agreed upon meeting times, communicate what this might look like. If texting or chat forums are acceptable, agree upon time constraints, if any. If you are agreeing to make yourself accessible to your mentee, determine that up front. Likewise, if you don't want this kind of continuous access, set up that rule at the beginning of the relationship. Generally, mentees will respect your time and limit their interruptions. Ensure you set expectations at the beginning of the relationship.

> Mentoring is more than creating your mini-me; it's about expanding the mentee's capabilities, and your own.

Mentoring creates growth opportunities for you in surprising ways. As you share your worldview on leadership and advise and support others, you'll have an excellent opportunity to refine your own thinking on leadership as you articulate and teach it. You'll find yourself thinking about your own leadership style in the context of what you're articulating and modeling to others. Mentoring is more than creating your mini-me; it's about expanding the mentee's capabilities, and your own.

Think also about what you can learn from your mentee. Sometimes the best lessons in leadership come from these meetings as you update your thinking about life experiences. For example, what is the young parent challenged with in the workplace? If you were a young parent twenty years ago, how have the stressors changed? How can this knowledge help you as you lead young teammates? What does your mentee believe the barriers to success are in your organization? The relationships you form can provide important insights to you about the workforce and the organizational culture as a whole.

Think of the people who've been influential in your career and consider why you remember them as having a place of importance in your success. As I remembered Night Shift Mary in an earlier chapter, I was reminded of an important mentor who impacted me from that same firm. He was a partner for whom I didn't work directly, but he knew the frustrations that Mary caused for her workforce. In order to keep us satisfied, motivated, growing, and dedicated to the firm, Dan would tap associates on Mary's team from time to time to work as our schedules allowed on cases that he was managing. He would ask if we were interested in a particular subject matter. While being respectful to Mary's time commitments on us, he would allow us to do what we could to get exposed to different aspects of law and procedure. Dan provided a relief valve, and he mentored and taught skills that I use still today. Looking back, the only thing I remember about working for Mary was the frustration. Nearly all my

The Secret Sauce

fond memories and the subject matter experience I gained from my time at that firm came from working on Dan's cases. Because of my benefit from Dan's example, today I look for people who may be trapped in areas where leadership seems lacking. I throw those people life rings, similar to what Dan did for me. I mentor and guide them to a better place, and help them "escape," as appropriate.

Find a mentor or mentors for yourself, too. Choose your own mentors well, and create goals that you'd like to meet as a result of your relationship. Find a solid mentor who can help you to grow. Perhaps there is a board member or another leader in the organization who you admire. Consider looking outside your organization as well. People generally are honored to impart their experiences to you and to share wisdom with others. Find someone who appreciates a curious mind, and then, like Jamie, take your own mentoring seriously as you strive to make being mentored a verb.

Commit to help people attain their dreams. I always begin mentoring relationships with one simple question: "What do you want to be when you grow up?" The answer requires introspection. As George Harrison sings, "If you don't know where you're going, any road will take you there." Our drive, compassion, excitement, and motivation come

> Commit to help people attain their dreams. I always begin mentoring relationships with one simple question: "What do you want to be when you grow up?"

from chasing dreams. These dreams are instilled in us at a young age, even before we can articulate them. Some people are never encouraged to name these dreams and reach for them. Leading well includes caring enough to help people identify and realize their dreams. Be prepared to share your own journey as you lead and mentor those within your scope of influence. Sharing your journey of success will inspire others to strive for their own.

No leader gets a pass in the mentoring department. Leading well and mentoring well go hand-in-hand. Think of those who've mentored you in formal or informal ways. As a leader, you are a person of influence. Make your influence count. As you lead well, you will teach others to model attributes that will teach, train, and encourage others to deliver exceptional results.

> "As iron sharpens iron, so one person sharpens another,"
>
> Proverbs 27:17.

Chapter 10
Hire Well

> *Commit to hire the **RIGHT** people with the right values and the right expertise. If you're the smartest person in the room, you're in the wrong room.*

Always hire people that enhance and improve the talent that already exists on the team. Surround yourself with the smartest people you can find and who share your organizational values and the values of your team. Every manager is responsible for certain deliverables and performance metrics of his or her assigned team. The smarter and more efficient the people you manage are, the better you can expect the overall potential and performance of the team to be.

Smart leaders hire people who are really talented and who have significant growth potential.

I remember one gentleman I interviewed for a mid-level financial position. He had impressive subject matter knowledge and was able to articulate his experience well. He was stuck in an organization that didn't value his potential, and he hadn't been promoted in several years. I could see from his interview his competence was above his title, and even above the position I was interviewing him for. He never disparaged his current employer or his lack of promotion. He was dedicated to the success of his current team, but the organization simply wasn't one that valued or even recognized his commitment. He was interviewing with me because he believed his organization was now pushing him into an area that ethically he believed was wrong. He was calm and matter of fact. I loved his competence and his strong moral center, and I hired him on the spot. Years (and several promotions) later, he proved to be one of the best hires I've ever made. We hired up with this gentleman, and he, along with the entire organization, benefitted.

> Thoughtfully bring people into the fold who enhance and improve the team from both a competency and a values perspective. One bad hire can ruin the culture of a cohesive team.

Look for people who bring the best of some quality to your team. Hire people who complement the existing members of the team and who bring in new concepts, new competencies, and new ideas. These talented hires will bring a new dynamic to your team and to the organization as a whole, and ultimately expand the competency of the entire team. Look for creativity, a willingness and track record of thinking differently, and situational experience that indicates they'll be successful on your team. My favorite hires are those very capable people who are stuck in an organization that has a substandard culture and who have great potential that no one is recognizing or grooming. Hire that person, invest in them, promote them, and your entire organization will benefit.

Your team's success depends on your ability to hire well. Bringing new people into the mix is one of the most important decisions leaders make. Thoughtfully bring people into the fold who enhance and improve the team from both a competency and a values perspective. One bad hire can ruin the culture of a cohesive team. Be able to articulate what is special about the culture of your team, and identify interview questions that allow you to identify candidates who share the values of your team.

> Hiring, interviewing and training takes time, but compare the output of the extremely qualified individual who wants to be promoted to that of an average employee.

Likewise, think about qualities you don't want on your team and fashion interview questions that will identify behaviors that are counter to the culture you're trying to build.

I've had managers tell me that they passed over candidates who they believed would join the company and only perform in the job for a few months because they were overqualified or otherwise extremely capable. The hiring manager feared these capable candidates would quickly be promoted to another department. They opted to overlook these qualified individuals. Instead, they chose to hire less qualified and less impressive teammates with the expectation the candidate would be content in the position for which they were hired. Hiring and interviewing and training take time, but compare the output of the extremely qualified individual who wants to be promoted to that of an average employee. A strong, confident leader will take the risk with the highly qualified individual. After all, you're building the value of the organization as a whole with these smart hires.

> The second you place your need to fill a position quickly over your need to fill it well, you've diminished the ability of the entire team, and you've made your ability to lead well that much harder.

One challenge faced by many managers is the temptation to believe that they are somehow superior in knowledge and savvy to the other members of the team. As the leader, do you genuinely believe you are the smartest member of the team? I hope not, because it's probably not true. If it is, you probably haven't hired very wisely. Strive to hire people who will make your team and your organization better from both a values and a competency perspective. Always hire up. Do a gut check on what drives you in a selection process for new teammates. Are you genuinely looking for values oriented, competent people who will expand the knowledge base of your team, or are you looking for people who will agree with you as their manager and just go with the flow?

The values held by an individual are key to the team's success. Some companies state their core values publicly. If yours does, you need to interview and hire people that share that belief system. Every company and every team has core values, even if those values aren't formally stated. Know the culture of the team you are leading, and then hire for shared values. Look for examples in an applicant's work history of successful teamwork. Don't drop your standards because it takes more time and effort to find quality people. Identify your best teammate and look for similar qualities in candidates. You may consider even involving that top performer in the interview process, or reward them for bringing in other top-notch teammates. Some of the best hires I've ever made were the friends, neighbors or even family members of the best people on the team. The second you place your need to fill a position quickly over your need to fill it well, you've diminished the ability of the entire team, and you've made your ability to lead well that much harder.

I remember interviewing a young man in his twenties who wanted a sales position with our organization.

He was currently employed and showed me examples of his success in his current organization. He clearly smashed all sales goals, but his resume showed he changed companies about once per year. He indicated he always met or exceeded sales goals, and his sales capabilities were obvious even in the interview. Something didn't seem just right with him, though. As we talked, we discussed his activity in sports in high school. He was successful in every sport he played, and he talked about his sports awards in tennis, golf, and swimming. He was accustomed to winning. In fact, he indicated he didn't have a lot of close friendships because he spent much of his time perfecting his individual performance in these sports. While I believed he would put up sales numbers, I doubted he would be a match for our values of serving one another and team results over individual results. I didn't hire him. I've watched him over the years on LinkedIn. He changes companies still about once per year. My experience has taught me that you can teach competence, but it's very difficult to teach values to adults who don't value others.

There are few compliments to the effectiveness of your leadership style than having staff promoted from your team. This will reflect well on you. This shows you know how to hire smart, mentor well, and that you encourage the growth of those you serve. And think of the things you'll learn from these smart people along the way! Don't fall into the trap of fearing that hiring smart and talented people will somehow make you look less effective. Smart team members make their hiring managers smarter. Hiring up is a great reflection on your confidence in your own capabilities and your security in your role.

Dare to look for people who don't think like you. Know the needs of your team and find people who bring a new perspective. If you have a dominant personality for example, consider hiring someone with a more analytical personality to complement your skill set. We are attracted personally and professional to people who are like us. You'll learn the most and accomplish the biggest goals if you strive to build a team of individuals with different personalities. Broad and diverse perspectives will push the entire origination further than a group of like-minded thinkers ever will.

The most challenging individual I ever added to my team was a highly educated, close-your-eyes-and-dream-with-me intellectual. The most accurate description I can provide is that he liked to follow sparkly things. I am a doer. I analyze, plan, and do. He was a dreamer. He dreams, dreams some more, and when the dream is so big you forgot the question, he dreams some more. However, because this gentleman saw the entire world differently than I did, he added a strategic flare to our team that inspired the entire team's creativity and innovation. It would have been easier to hire someone into his role who had the same personality type as me. We perhaps would have even accomplished a lot, but we wouldn't have been as creative, and when we moved past the dream stage into execution, when a vision became operational, it was incredible. He was difficult to lead well, but together we delivered exceptional results.

> Dare to hire people who aspire to grow. Hire up for values and competency and you'll create a superior team of folks who will deliver exceptional results to your customers.

It's even more important to hire up in entry-level positions. Dare to hire people who aspire to grow. Hire up for values and competency and you'll create a superior team of folks who will deliver exceptional results to your customers. Imagine the impact of a highly motivated team of people in entry-level jobs. Imagine a fast food team where the manager, leading well, creates training opportunities in which the highest performers learn different skills, preparing them for a promotion. Imagine the impact of a formal mentoring program on a team like this. Imagine the effectiveness of promoting one of these highly motivated teammates within your department. Imagine the customer service that will be provided by people who genuinely love what they are doing because they know they are appreciated and encouraged to grow.

Contrast that with an entire team of people who work for a paycheck, until the next opportunity to make a quarter more an hour comes along. That team may well be dependable, but it will be difficult to improve their service to your customer if they aren't committed to performance in the seat they are in. Hire up for values or competency or both.

Beware of pride when you enter into the hiring process. Far too many leaders allow personal pride to prevent them from expanding the competency of their team. Check yourself by considering what you believe your best professional skill or characteristic to be. Let's say you believe you are a marketing genius. Do you look to hire young, innovative talent that has new perspectives on this rapidly changing field, knowing others may see them as the new marketing genius of the team? Or do you see new talent as an opportunity to expand the knowledge base of marketing for your team, even if someone else dethrones you as the genius? Perhaps you believe you're a charismatic leader, and the team will follow your lead whatever direction you take them. When hiring new leaders for your organization, do you look for strong, capable leaders with a track record for leading well? Or are you afraid of someone new rising above you in the ranks? Pride is often not only the downfall of great individuals, but it can be the downfall of great organizations when it causes poor decisions to be made for the purpose of preserving an individual's perceived self-worth. Hire up, and that includes in the areas where your competency is high.

Recognize the hidden talents and growing competencies of people within the organization when you are hiring up. In most organizations, there are a variety of people at different stages of educational growth. It's not uncommon for adults to be in college programs, often in fields of competency different than the job they currently hold. There is considerable value in hiring people with organizational knowledge into roles that may match their new training and education. One young man comes to mind. He was working full-time in an entry-level call center position and attending night school full-time for a healthcare management degree. When he was close to graduation, he came to ask my advice. He wondered if he should leave our organization to seek a leadership position. He doubted he could make a move from an entry-level job in our call center to a leadership position in the operations division of our organization. He wondered if he would be respected or always seen as a member of the call center team. I thought it spoke volumes about this young man that he worked successfully full-time in the call center, and while he was in school full time he didn't act as though the job was beneath him. He wasn't just passing through. Quite the opposite—he didn't talk about being in school, and most of his peers didn't know he was working on the degree. He provided great service to our customers, showed an excellent work ethic, and knowing that he juggled job and school, showed an aptitude to carry a heavy load. I considered him an excellent candidate for a management position in our organization. His years working with our customers gave him great insights and allowed him to have an excellent understanding of the complexities of our organization. He would bring a great perspective to the operations team. We hired him into a management position, and he proved to be a great internal example of hiring up.

Hiring well means hiring the best people to fill the needs of your organization and upgrading the skills that are on the team today. Think about the needs of the organization, your customers, and your team, and hire the best talent you can find. If you foster an environment of continuous improvement, the team as a whole will appreciate the value hiring well brings to everyone. If you are practicing the other ingredients we've already discussed in earlier chapters, your team won't be threatened by hires that bring new competency to the team. Integrate new members by welcoming them in the same way you serve the existing team. Your team will appreciate your efforts to hire well for exceptional results.

> One bad hire that compromises the values of the team can reverse years of building a culture you've been committed to. One bad hire can compromise years of success. One bad hire can cause an exodus of people who've been committed performers for a long time.

Leading well and hiring well go hand in hand. Every person you hire onto the team should reflect the vision and leadership style you are living each day. One bad hire that compromises the values of the team can reverse years of building a culture you've been committed to. One bad hire can compromise years of success. One bad hire can cause an exodus of people who've been committed performers for a long time. Leading well means waiting for the right hire, for the good of the team.

> "Where there is strife, there is pride, but wisdom is found in those who take advice,"

Proverbs 13:10.

Post Script
Resist Bone-Headed Strategy

So we're right back where we started. With that friend from the restaurant management world who shared a great insight with me. "You can have the best marketing plan in the world to launch a new restaurant chain," she said, "but if the food isn't good, it won't matter." Bad leadership can ruin a business that's running well. The most charismatic, authentic, inspiring, motivated servant leader will only be able to lead a team for so long when strategic thinking regarding where the business is headed misses the mark.

What you know about the business you are leading, and how you drive the decisions that will impact your team, matters. Decisions made from a place of misplaced pride or greed will dissolve any progress you've made growing the engagement of a team. If you do make a strategic mistake, admit it, change it, and move on. Don't double down on bad judgment to cover your tracks. Your team is depending on you to think of their well-being before you think of your own. You can do this, or you wouldn't be in the pages of this book.

Leading well really is the secret sauce of any successful organization. You simply cannot sustain growth, success, and satisfaction with bad leadership. As a leader, I consider it joy that I have the opportunity to inspire and encourage those around me every day. I look for ways to build others up in everything I do. I have learned that people who are empowered, appreciated, and respected strive to do well and deliver exceptional results. They have a hop in their step and a drive in their spirit and they enjoy coming to the workplace. They devour their assignments and complete them with energy and enthusiasm. Being a leader who motivates others is great for business. It's also the only way to build sustainable success. People are the greatest asset in any organization. Imagine the impact of an entire workforce who feels appreciated and inspired to deliver their best. They'll not only deliver exceptional results, they'll emulate the inspirational style that is motivating them, and they'll motivate others. Leading well is contagious. And everyone will want the recipe to the secret sauce.

If you follow this secret sauce recipe, I'm confident you will see improved employee engagement and improved organizational results as you lead well. You will also have the satisfaction of creating a work environment that honors and inspires others. To be entrusted to lead others where they spend more working hours than anywhere else is an honor. That you understand the importance of the honor, and desire to serve others, says volumes about your character.

Good luck, and lead well! As you apply the Secret Sauce to your organization, please share your stories of success with me at www.dottybollinger.com!

About The Author

As a healthcare executive and evangelical Christian, Dotty J Bollinger has boldly served the Lord in the secular marketplace for nearly three decades. She attributes her professional achievements to the spiritual foundation on which she has built her career. Driven by conviction, she is passionate about leading well, mentoring, and coaching team members towards their kingdom success in the marketplace and at home.

As a nurse and an attorney, Dotty has served as SVP of Risk Management and General Counsel for Horizon Bay Senior Communities. Most recently she has held the position of President and Chief Operating Officer for Laser Spine Institute. Dotty and her husband, Jim, serve healthcare practices all over the United States with their consulting firm.

Dotty and Jim are parents to daughters Ashley, Sara, and son-in-law Kevin, and live joyfully in Gatlinburg, Tennessee. When they aren't traveling the nation assisting healthcare clients, Jim is enjoying pursuing part-time law school "for the fun of it" and Dotty is writing books. In their free time they find rejuvenation and inspiration by being active in their church, hiking, camping, cross-country skiing, working the land, and enjoying the breathtaking views from their cabin in the majestic Smoky Mountains. Find Dotty at www.dottybollinger.com, or join us on social media on Facebook (Dotty J Bollinger), Twitter @ DottyBollinger, and LinkedIn.

Check out Dotty's first book, Women of Faith In The Marketplace: Finding Your Kingdom Purpose, Friesen Press, 2016.